Unhealthy Places

Unhealthy Places

The Ecology of Risk
in the Urban Landscape

Kevin Fitzpatrick and Mark LaGory

ROUTLEDGE • New York • London

Published in 2000 by
Routledge
29 West 35th Street
New York, NY 10001

Published in Great Britain by
Routledge
11 New Fetter Lane
London EC4P 4EE

Printed in the United States of America on acid-free paper.
Design and typography: Cynthia Dunne

Library of Congress Cataloging-in-Publication Data
Fitzpatrick, Kevin M.
Unhealthy places : the ecology of risk in the urban landscape /
Kevin M. Fitzpatrick, Mark E. LaGory
p.   cm.
Includes bibliographical references and index.
ISBN 0-415-92371-9 (hb). — ISBN 0-415-92372-7 (pb)
1. Inner cities—Health aspects—United States. 2. Urban poor—Health
and hygiene—United States. I. LaGory, Mark, 1947-
II. Title.
RA566. 3.F58 2000   99-42750
362. 1'09173'2—dc21   CIP

To my family—my parents, William and Evelyn, my brother, Jim, and his family, my children, Amanda, Aaron, and Michael, and my wife, Mary. I dedicate this book to all of you. Your love and support have played a vital role in this project in ways that are impossible for me to measure.

—Kevin Fitzpatrick

To all people in need, mindful not only of their needs but of the gifts they can give, and to my family, who gives enouragement and support.

—Mark LaGory

Contents

List of Tables/Figures

Acknowledgments

This book began to take shape nearly twenty years ago when the first author took his first graduate course in urban sociology from Mark LaGory. Since then an extremely fruitful and vibrant professional and personal relationship has evolved, enabling this project to be both enjoyable and intellectually satisfying.

We would like to acknowledge the support, assistance, insight, criticism, and thoughtful reflection of several people and organizations important to the development of this project. We would like to thank the University of Alabama at Birmingham, School of Social and Behavioral Sciences, and the Department of Sociology for creating an intellectual environment that encourages cross-disciplinary thinking with real-world applications. Specifically, we acknowledge the support and leadership provided by our dean, Tennant McWilliams and our chair, William Cockerham. We would also like to thank Sean-Shong Hwang, Bronwen Lichtenstein, and William Yoels for reading various sections of the manuscript and providing helpful suggestions for its improvement. We are indebted to William Michelson from the University of Toronto, whose review provided us keen theoretical insight and interdisciplinary knowledge that helped broaden the scope of the book while at the same time sharpening its final message.

For expertise on specific areas we would like to thank Acklaque Hacque, UAB Center for Urban Affairs, who provided us with GIS-based census data on the Village Creek area; Richard Sinsky, Jefferson County Department of Health, who gave us access to critical health data on the Village Creek neighborhoods; and both Jim Fenstermaker, Birmingham Department of Planning, and Robert Montgomery, Greater Birmingham Ministries, for providing us with key insights into the plight of Village Creek neighborhoods.

A special thanks to our research assistants, Debra Carrier, Michael Foti, Darlene Wright, and Tiffany Martin for their help through various phases of this project. In addition, we would like to express our appreciation to the staff at Routledge, our editor, Ilene Kalish, editorial assistant, Shea Settimi, and production editor, Jennifer Hirshlag, for making what seemed like a monumental task a doable one.

Finally, we would like to single out and thank our wives, Mary and Mary Sue, for the many roles they play, their encouragement, and their love and support, without which this project would not have been possible.

The Importance of Place

Like those of other living things, our structure, development, and behavior arise from a genetic foundation sunk in an environmental context. Yet while we readily accept that a healthy seed can't grow into a plant without the right soil, air, light and water, and that a feral dog won't behave like a pet, we resist recognizing the importance of environment in our own lives.

WINIFRED GALLAGHER

lames leapt 200 feet into the air. A thick pillar of black smoke loomed over the city as a fire, punctuated by a series of explosions, consumed a six-acre warehouse complex in downtown Birmingham, Alabama, on October 2, 1997. The warehouse, which burned for three days, contained large concentrations of hazardous chemicals. A 15-square-block area near the warehouse was evacuated because of the health risks to persons in the vicinity. Hours after the fire started, black particles continued to rain down from the sky onto the clothing and skin of pedestrians in the

downtown area. Millions of gallons of water used to douse the fire
flooded the sewer system and washed into Village Creek, a stream that
periodically floods low-income neighborhoods on the western side of
Birmingham, near the downtown.

Uncertainty surrounding the dangers posed by the fire and by pollutants released into the air and water continued for nearly a week after
the fire began. Initially, state and county officials denied that hazardous
materials had leaked from the warehouse. As early as the day following
the fire's start, however, newspapers reported that nearly 5,000 gallons
of a highly concentrated form of Dursban (80 times the over-the-
counter concentration) had been released into the water and air.
Dursban is an organophosphate pesticide, a low-level nerve agent,
believed to cause acute and chronic health problems ranging from birth
defects, chronic headaches and neuromuscular pain, short-term memory
loss, nausea and vomiting, and breathing problems, to a condition
known as multiple chemical sensitivity (U.S. Environmental Protection
Agency 1997). Concerns over the safety of Dursban raised by the
Environmental Protection Agency (EPA) led its manufacturer, Dow
Chemical, to voluntarily restrict its marketing and revise instructions
for application and use.

In the first few days after the fire began, residents living in the low-
income, mainly African-American neighborhoods near Village Creek
reported smelling noxious fumes and experiencing a variety of physical
symptoms including headaches and nausea. Dying fish and other signs
of serious environmental problems were noticed in the stream that flows
through their neighborhoods. It took almost a week, however, before
any official response to residents' complaints occurred. Six days after the
fire, "no fishing" signs were posted in the area, and test results on water
and air samples were finally released by the Alabama Department of
Environmental Management. By then, the seriousness of the contamination was obvious. Village Creek had become a flowing stream of dead,
rotting fish. Residents living along the creek complained to EPA lawyers
about the slow response of local officials to their concerns. They
believed that the spill would have been taken more seriously if the damage had occurred in a better-off neighborhood where residents were
mostly White. Indeed, it was only after the polluted waters began to
wreak devastation further downstream, near those better-off residential

areas, that more serious precautionary measures were taken. A temporary filtration dam was built to protect these areas from pollutants, but it failed. In a span of three weeks, almost 30 miles of waterway near residential areas were contaminated and hundreds of thousands of fish killed. The first legal actions were taken only after pollution began to wash ashore near higher-income, mostly White residential areas. Civil suits were filed on behalf of local residents in two of these areas (a residential area near Bay View Lake and one near the Black Warrior River). These suits raised concerns about damage to the water supply and impact on housing values.

Six months after the fire and the largest Dursban spill in history, contamination levels in some areas remained high, although the waterways showed signs of a slow recovery. While a number of reports of medical problems connected with Dursban poisoning have been reported to the County Health Department, little is known about the long-term public health consequences of the spill. Despite media coverage, surprisingly little consideration has been given to the mental health consequences of the event in the Village Creek area. This spill represented a dramatic ecological event, but it was only one instance in a long history of environmental problems. Village Creek is a dumping ground for industrial waste and is prone to other environmental problems such as periodic flooding. Residence here is stressful. The chronic nature of this stress hit home shortly after the fire, when those living along the creek reported strange smells and dramatic changes in the waterway's color; the problems turned out to be a result of industrial pollution from a nearby business. Just another day along Village Creek!

The natural history of this disaster is representative of a larger public health issue in the United States. Persons living nearest to the city center, in areas with large concentrations of poor minorities, are exposed to serious physical and mental health risks (Andrulis 1997; Greenberg 1991). With limited resources to address these risks, residents have found existing agencies incapable or unwilling to deal with the wide range of problems encountered. Risky environments are not usually the ones where politically effective responses occur or where the greatest public efforts are made to address the problem. Yet, in this ineffective response to serious health needs, the health and well-being of the greater whole is affected. As Dr. Martin Luther King Jr. once reminded us: "Of all the forms of inequality, injustice in health is the most shocking and the most inhumane."

Place Matters

Place is a key element in our identity. Who we are is reflected in the places we occupy and the spaces we control. These places range from nation to region, state, metropolitan area, community, neighborhood, block, and residential dwelling. Each location has profound social meaning for us, and in a literal sense defines not only who we are, but also how we live and die.

Despite the evolution of cyberspace technologies capable of transforming "theres" into "heres," residence continues to have dramatic consequences for individual health and well-being. The prevalence and incidence of risks for a variety of physical and mental health conditions within metropolitan areas range widely by residential area. Most notably, life and death experiences in the inner city are more similar to people in the Third World than to the experience of suburbanites just a few miles away. Perhaps the most notorious examples of this situation are the neighborhoods of Harlem in New York City and Roxbury in Boston. Mortality rates in these places for Black men under 65 are more than double the rates of U.S. Whites and 50 percent higher than the rates for all U.S. Blacks (McCord and Freeman 1990).

For certain segments of the population, being in the wrong place is not a matter of timing or accident, *but rather a function of the social structure*. The places we live, work, and play in are fundamental resources, like time or money. The access we have to these resources dramatically affects our well-being. All human beings live in a spatial world where everything and everybody has its place. Everyday lives are spatially structured. At the heart of this structure is a simple fact—there is distance between ourselves and the other actors and objects in our environment. To satisfy basic needs and interests we must find ways of getting objects or actors we have an interest in to either come to us, or find ways of getting to them. Hence, where people live is of great importance.

Place matters in the contemporary world, but for different reasons than in the past. Our ancestors were place-bound by necessity. Indeed, for most of human life on earth we lived as hunters and gatherers, living off the land in small bands so isolated from each other that strangers were met with great suspicion and alarm.

> The accounts of early European voyagers to out-of-the-way parts of the globe tell again and again of their being received by the native populations with fear, astonishment, apprehension, ceremonies of propitiation, protective rituals, fainting, and so forth—the exact emotion and behavior of the hosts depending on just what they conceived these strange white objects to be. (Lofland 1973:5)

Dramatic technological revolutions eroded this isolation in ever intensifying waves of change—first, an agricultural revolution 10,000 years ago, then an industrial-urban revolution 9,700 years later. During this vast period of time, the spatial horizons of people broadened as transportation and communication technologies improved, trade expanded, and cities attracted large numbers of culturally heterogeneous populations. We are now in the midst of a microelectronics revolution. This third wave of change is technically capable of ending the isolation between people; yet spatial barriers persist in this post-industrial world where highly segregated cities contain distinct inner-city and outer-city areas. Thus, as we enter a new millennium, space is redefined and reshaped, and for some takes on a new level of significance.

The enduring significance of place is truly remarkable, for technologies now exist to move people and materials vast distances in very short times, while information can be transported almost instantaneously to the most remote regions of the world. Distant places have attained a "hereness" nearly unimaginable a century ago. Marshall McLuhan (1965) describes this new world as a "global village," but this place has a more distant potential for certain segments of the population. Indeed, when surveying the urban geography, with its vast neighborhood differentials in health risks, the more appropriate spatial analogy may be that of an expanding universe of places moving farther away from each other, rather than closer.

There is good news and bad news contained in the reality of evolutionary trends. While technological developments in transportation, communication, and information processing give humans new capacities to break down spatial barriers, a socially structured spatial environment produces new barriers. These structures are the modern-day equivalent of the medieval city's walls—separating portions of society from one another and preserving vast differences in levels of living and overall well-being. Awareness of the impact of these invisible barriers for the health and well-being of large numbers in our society may make it possible to develop programs to alleviate this spatial penalty. As Melvin Webber has suggested (1964), we have the technological capacity to live in a "nonplace urban realm" where the friction of distance is minimized. At present, however, we live in a bifurcated world of possibility and actuality. There is the potential for a nonplace urban realm, but at the same time there is the reality of a highly segregated city perpetuating an ecology of disadvantage.

While the greatest disadvantages in the urban area clearly accrue to residents of the inner city, place-bound risks are not unique to the ghetto. Urban sprawl on the edge of the metropolis has produced places of numbing "sameness" with no identity or sense of community. The recent rash of suburban school shootings has led some observers to conclude that there may be conditions unique to suburbs that place certain vulnerable groups at risk, particularly youth. A recent *New York Times* article suggests that suburban design may be failing to provide a safe haven for younger residents.

> As quickly as the word "alienation" can be attached to the idea of youth, the image of isolation can be attached to the picture of suburbs. Is there an unexplored relationship between them? It is a question parents and urban planners are raising in the aftermath of the Columbine High School shootings in Littleton, Colorado. At a time when the renegade sprawl of suburbs themselves is being intensely scrutinized, the troubling vision of a nation re-pioneered in vast tracts of disconnected communities has produced uneasy discussion about the psychological disorientation they might house. (Hamilton 1999)

Why an Urban, Place-Based Approach to Health?

There is an ecology of disadvantage in America, and one of its most significant outcomes is the "urban health penalty" (Greenberg 1991). This penalty is important to understand for several reasons. First, we live in an urban society. While a century ago only 25 percent of the population resided in urban areas, now roughly three-fourths live in a metropolitan area consisting of one or more central cities and a ring of suburbs. Second, experts generally agree that the single most important global environmental influence in this century, and for the foreseeable future, is the process of urbanization itself (Gallagher 1993). Today, a little more than 40 percent of the world's population lives in cities, but if world urbanization trends continue, it is estimated that roughly 25 years from now more than two-thirds of the world will be urban (Brockerhoff 1996). The impact on the ecosystem of such an event would be catastrophic, with dramatic increases in pollution, consumption of nonrenewable resources and irretrievable losses of millions of known and unknown animal and plant species (Meadows et al. 1972). Third, the city is a distinct social environment that over time has accentuated great inequities between peoples. Within its boundaries dramatic variation exists in material wealth, personal well-being, and overall quality of life. Finally, the city is an artificially constructed environment, an "intentional" or "built" environment, and thus it can be reengineered to promote more desirable health outcomes. Unlike natural disasters, the disasters befalling some of our inner cities are preventable.

Andrulis (1997) highlights a series of indicators suggesting the health costs of urban residence, particularly residence in one part of the city—the inner city. Among the most striking observations are:

- Residents in the 100 largest cities in the United States fall victim to violence twice as often as others. Murder rates are more than twice as high.

- The infant mortality rate in the 100 largest cities is 25 percent higher than the U.S. average.

- Of the 880 most disadvantaged neighborhoods identified by the Child Welfare League, 99 percent were located in cities.

- Forty percent of urban children live below the poverty level.

- Gang-related homicides rose from 18 percent of total killings in Los Angeles in 1979 to 43 percent in 1994.

- Thirty percent to 50 percent of city children are inadequately immunized.

- The mortality rate for urban children increased by 50 percent between 1980 and 1988.

The health of inner-city residents is significantly worse than in other places in the United States. In the inner city, the circumstances of poverty and minority status are exacerbated by segregation; the spatial concentration of these two characteristics apparently intensifies the disadvantages of low income and minority status. Indeed, the American College of Physicians concludes: "One of the most important characteristics [of the health care challenge] is the interrelationships among health and social and environmental problems. The so-called 'urban health penalty'—the confluence of circumstances such as poor nutrition, poverty and unemployment with deteriorating housing, violence and loss of services—has created a deepening health crisis in the inner city." A medical approach, in other words, can no longer be sufficient to reduce the differentials that exist in American health because health risks are spatially and socially structured. Indeed, there is growing realization within medicine and public health that societal forces actually shape and create the disease patterns experienced by a society, and that successful health interventions require addressing the social factors that produce them (Link and Phelan 1996). Place is a critical social factor.

While the concepts of place and environment are essential to understanding physical and mental health outcomes in society, they are rather broad, multidimensional constructs. Place can be defined as a portion of space regarded as measured off or distinct from other spaces. It can be conceptualized as a position or site in space. The environment can be thought of as the totality of surrounding conditions, as an area in which something exists. Both concepts imply a force, which is more than physical in character. As an environment, a place can be seen as a container whose characteristics derive primarily from what is contained within its recognized boundaries. These contents involve physical, cultural, and social components.

As a point or portion of space, spatial coordinates can define a place, and hence it has physical qualities. But it is also a space which is socially, culturally, economically, politically, and psychologically defined. The places occupied by individuals are thus not just physical entities characterized by physical positions in space or by the characteristics of those elements contained within the spaces. They are also mental constructs, psychologically defined by individuals who possess culture and occupy certain positions within society. Each person carries around a set of mental maps that are a product of personal experiences, cultural stereotypes, preferences, objective information, and so on. We live in personal worlds, so that the very same places may be understood and defined very differently by persons with different sociocultural backgrounds and personal experiences. One person's heaven may be another's hell. Understanding the relationship between environment and health thus requires a careful analysis of environments in all their complexity, for place is a multidimensional construct.

The Inner City: A Definition

Although this book deals with the impact of place in general on health, a major focus is on the inner city and its importance for the health of its residents. The term *inner city* is used frequently in both the popular and scientific literature on cities, yet it is seldom formally defined. In recent years this term has replaced earlier designations such as "slum" or "ghetto" as the social science catchphrase used to denote the spatial concentration of minority poverty in the nation's large cities. Perhaps the closest thing to a formal designation for the spatial concentration of minority poverty is contained in the work of urban researchers such as Wilson (1996) or Jargowsky and Bane (1991), who use U.S. census data to designate "ghetto poverty census tracts." Ghetto poverty areas are census tracts within Metropolitan Statistical Areas (MSA) where the household incomes of at least 40 percent of residents are below the poverty line. Researchers have noted three significant trends in these ghetto areas over the last several decades: 1) the number of ghetto areas more than doubled during the 1970s and 1980s; 2) the ratio of poor to nonpoor in ghetto areas increased dramatically; and 3) the African-American presence in ghetto tracts grew substantially (Wilson 1996). Today, nearly half of metropolitan area Blacks live in ghetto tracts that increasingly isolate the metropolitan Black poor from Whites and nonpoor Blacks.

While there is considerable debate over the issue (Massey and Denton 1993), Wilson (1980, 1987, 1996) believes that the growing concentration of Black poor in ghetto tracts represents a new trend in urban minority poverty. Wilson argues that the recent trends in ghetto poverty tracts are more than just an outgrowth of the processes of racial and class segregation. He believes that as jobs left the central city during the 1970s and 1980s, so did nonpoor Blacks, and as jobs and middle-class Blacks left, both the ghetto economy and ghetto community collapsed. He contends that the current concentration of minority poor occurs faster and for different reasons, and therefore uses the term "inner city" to replace the more traditional terms of ghetto and slum. Ghettos and slums, while products of dramatic racial segregation, were more organizationally stable since they contained a wide range of economic institutions and a sizable population of nonpoor who served in positions of leadership in the community.

> Though they may have lived on different streets, blacks of all classes in inner-city areas . . . lived in the same community and shopped at the same stores. Their children went to the same schools and played in the same parks. Although there was some class antagonism, their neighborhoods were more stable than the inner-city neighborhoods of today; in short, they featured higher levels of what social scientists call "social organization." (Wilson 1996:20)

We adopt Wilson's usage of *inner city* throughout this book, although the term ghetto poverty tract is more technically accurate. While the term *inner city* is currently fashionable, its use here does not necessarily signal acceptance of Wilson's analysis of urban minority poverty. Chapters 3 and 6 provide detailed discussion of different perspectives on the geographic concentration of deprivation in American cities.

Place as Life Chance and Risk

Every place we live in has certain levels of *hazard* and *risk* associated with its various social, cultural, and physical components. A hazard is a situation that, under particular circumstances, could lead to damage or harm to a human being or a population. It is thus a collection of situations and circumstances. An example might be the situation of a curving, deteriorating road which, under the circumstances of heavy traffic and light rain, could result in a multicar accident. Or in the case of the Birmingham warehouse fire, the situation was an unprotected stream, Village Creek, which frequently received runoff from the industries located around it. The circumstances which, in combination with this situation, led to the potential for serious environmental damage and human loss were: 1) a warehouse without adequate fire safety features, 2) heavy concentrations of dangerous chemicals stored in that warehouse, and 3) a metropolitan area and state with an ill-prepared emergency response team. Risk is defined as: "the probability of damage or harm in a specified period [and place]" (Royal Society Study Group 1992:3). In essence, risk is the likelihood of a hazard causing harm to an individual or population.

Beck (1995) has argued that risk and hazard are of particular importance in advanced modern societies ("risk societies") where a system of rules has developed to deal with industrially produced risks and insecurities. The calculus of risk, developed in the work of physical scientists, engineers, and public health professionals, has become the "mathematical morality of the technological age." In this form of reckoning, the risk of a decision or activity is calculated as a mathematical probability and is no longer defined as potential harm to individual human beings. That is, risks are borne by a population rather than by individuals. After scientists calculate risks, they are judged to be either more or less acceptable, and strategies are devised to contain risk within some acceptable range.

> Statistical documentation reveals these consequences as events conditioned by the system, and accordingly, in need of general political regulation. . . . A field is opened for corresponding political action: accidents on the job, for instance, are not blamed on those whose health they have already ruined anyway but are tied to the plant's organization, precautions, and so on. (Beck 1995:21–22)

Once risks are established, a series of protections can theoretically be devised to reduce the probabilities of harm or loss attached to certain decisions and the circumstances that surround them. In an advanced, high-technology society such risks can be very high. Some people will be more affected by the growth of these risks than others; that is, what Beck (1995) calls "social risk positions" develop which follow the inequalities of place and class standing. In the "risk society," levels of hazard and risk are differentially distributed in the urban landscape, and the distribution of risk and hazard in turn differentially affects health outcomes. Each level of residential place from nation to region, state, metropolitan area, community, neighborhood, block, and dwelling can be assessed in terms of health risks and hazards.

Places are environments consisting of physical, cultural, political, economic, and social components, with each component contributing in complex ways to the differential risks experienced by a population. At one level, place can be seen as a means of objectifying the complex set of risks that come together to affect a population's health—in short, a method for reporting health risk data. But it is clearly more than just a unit by which the health of a population can be reported and analyzed. Place is a meaningful unit, not simply because a population uses various places as the stage on which to carry out its behaviors and actions, but because the stage (or place) itself shapes these actions and experiences. We are who we are, and we experience what we do on a daily basis in part because of where we find ourselves. Our physical and mental health is a product of not only how we live, but also where we live.

Environments are *risk spaces*. The most obvious place-based health risks are associated with physical aspects of an environment. These include such things as harmful chemical agents, pollutants, viruses, and bacteria contained in a local space as well as the quality and arrangement of built and natural physical features in a place (architecture, building deterioration, building materials, landscape, etc.) that may present seen and unseen hazards for the occupants. But places also contain psychological and social risks as well. Some areas are decidedly more stressful, with too much noise, too many people, or just an overload of stimuli. Other places expose individuals to strangers where interactions are less secure and predictable, or to situations where hostile, aggressive interactions are possible. In many cases, the risks associated with place are heavily concentrated in just a few areas. Not surprisingly, such areas tend to occur where residents are least equipped to respond to the challenges imposed by place—such as Village Creek in Birmingham, the Roxbury area of Boston, or New York's Harlem.

Place as Social Resource

Just as the areas of a city can be viewed as risk spaces containing differing levels of hazard, cities are *resource spaces* where the goods and services capable of protecting inhabitants from harm are also differentially distributed. That is, cities have both a topography of risk and protection. This topography, as Beck (1995) notes, tends to follow the shape and structure of the larger society, with the most visible distinctions occurring at the opposite ends of the system of stratification. Each metropolitan area reflects the contours of the society, with risk heavily concentrated in the inner zones of the metropolis where there are significant concentrations of low-income, underemployed minorities. At the same time, protection from risk, in terms of availability of health professionals, community resources, and supportive social networks, tends to be inversely related to risk and risk locations. These are not merely matters of material differences between people but reflect a larger fabric of inequality only partially related to income. This inequality has become more obvious as the geography of inequality has become more apparent in America's cities. Historically, slums were so successfully hidden from the daily activities of middle-class consumers of the city space that they seemed nonexistent. Indeed, the term *slum* is believed to derive from the word *slumber,* because slums were composed of "unknown, back streets or alleys, wrongly presumed to be sleeping or quiet" (Partridge 1958). While patterns of residential segregation still permit most metropolitan residents to avoid slums on a daily basis, the geographical spread of the inner city and its multiplicity of problems make such places hard to ignore. They are certainly not sleeping or quiet, and the long-term implications of such concentrated risk for the society as a whole are significant.

Wilson (1996), in his discussion of the inner city, notes a substantial change in the character of the areas where minority poverty concentrates. Lower levels of "social organization" characterize the inner-city neighborhoods of today. He notes several optimal dimensions of neighborhood social organization: 1) the prevalence, strength, and interlocking of social networks; 2) the degree to which neighbors take personal responsibility for neighborhood problems; 3) the extent of surveillance done by neighbors; and 4) the degree of participation in formal and voluntary organizations tied to the neighborhood and to the larger community. Social organization in this sense is a critical protection against hazard and risk. Areas where there is a concentration of weak social networks, limited feelings of personal responsibility for neighbors, low levels of surveillance, and limited participation in the institutional network of the community are also areas where vulnerability to the risk of environmental hazard is concentrated. This susceptibility to risk becomes all the more important in areas with limited economic and political resources and high levels of hazard to begin with. The risks themselves are cumulative; that is, the hazardous nature of a given environmental circumstance intensifies under the absence of protection. Strong organizational structures in an area can serve as a form of inoculation against stress and ill health. Neighborhood context can promote a culture of vigilance and responsibility that mitigates against local hazards and risk, while at the same time empowering individuals to take action against the hazards present in local spaces.

Place is a force in the lives and health of a population apart from the individuals and risks associated with that place; it is a real factor in personal well-being. Individual choices and actions take place in spaces which in turn shape and structure those choices and actions. Places are the stages upon which social and cultural forces in the larger society affect individuals. In this sense, the spatial division between inner-city areas and the rest of the metropolis is a reflection of the U.S. society's structure itself; the spatial distance between populations reflects their social distance, their position within the larger society (LaGory and Pipkin 1981). The existence of the inner city is geographic testimony to the dramatic socioeconomic divide that persists between certain minority groups (most notably African Americans and Hispanics) and mainstream America. Cities from their very origins were founded on differences, just as the societies which contained them involved a system of stratification. In preindustrial cities, these differences were primarily between the urban resident and the peasants. Walls were erected to regulate access to the city's resources and to protect the system of differences that prevailed in society. The social distance between citizen and peasant was dramatically symbolized and reinforced by the city walls. The contemporary city is heterogeneous, yet real barriers exist between residents.

The contemporary city's walls are not like the physical structures of the preindustrial city, but there are real physical and mentally constructed barriers between the populations that reside there. The barriers are reflected in pervasive patterns of segregation, with those groups at the bottom of the social system most highly segregated from others. As groups assimilate into the larger society they are less likely to be concentrated in certain areas and tend to disperse across the urban landscape. This does not mean, however, that minority groups which scatter across the metropolis are any less likely to be segregated. For example, while middle-class African Americans have dispersed spatially they remain highly segregated from Whites. Massey and Denton (1993) note that the most significant feature of the U.S. postwar residential pattern has been the concentration of Blacks in central cities and Whites in suburbs. While Black suburbanization has occurred, only a small percentage of Blacks live in suburbs, and most of those live in highly segregated, older suburbs.

Segregation is a powerful spatial force that serves to protect the status quo, and it separates groups from one another. Highly segregated groups find themselves isolated from the organizational structures and resources necessary to promote health and well-being.

> Unless ghetto residents work outside of their neighborhoods, they are unlikely to come into contact with anyone else who is not also black, and if they live in concentrated poverty, they are unlikely to interact with anyone who is not also poor and black. (Massey and Denton 1993:160)

Thus, segregation ensures that neighborhoods with limited resources for protection against risk will be particularly vulnerable since their isolation restricts their access to the range of resources available in the larger community. Places with weak social organization that are also highly segregated promote an existence very different from the rest of the society. This type of segregation creates walls as real and impermeable as those in ancient preindustrial cities.

Insularity is likely to promote cultural differences across the urban landscape as well. Places in which outside contact is restricted become fertile ground for the promotion of subcultures and lifestyles associated with high-risk behaviors. There is strong evidence that pursuing a healthy lifestyle can enhance health and life expectancy (Cockerham 1998). It is also well-known that certain lifestyles have negative health consequences. Unprotected sex, promiscuous sexuality, and intravenous drug use increase the risk of contracting AIDS. Smoking is linked to lung cancer and heart disease, alcoholism to cirrhosis of the liver. Participation in gangs increases the exposure to violence and risk of physical injury, while high-fat diets accelerate the risk of heart disease and atherosclerosis. Segregation may be linked to the promotion of unhealthy lifestyles by creating the conditions in which access to mainstream role models are highly constrained and access to deviant institutions and deviant subculture are intensified. In criminology, differential association theory (Sutherland and Cressey 1960; Taylor 1988) suggests that individuals develop deviant lifestyles because of their exposure to certain contexts. Certain lifestyles, in other words, are more likely to be learned because individuals in highly segregated settings experience greater exposure to deviant subcultures and greater isolation from more traditional health lifestyles.

Besides promoting subcultural differences in health lifestyles, segregation can enhance the negative circumstances of already stressful inner-city environments. Since the mental well-being of individuals undergoing stress is in part a function of their social resources, it stands to reason that the range of these resources will have an impact on health. People living in spatially constrained communities have spatially constrained support systems, and hence may be more likely to experience the negative consequences of stress (Haines and Hurlbert 1992).

The Multidimensional Nature of Place

The neighborhood is an important place for the provision of protection against risk, and much of our discussion focuses on that spatial level. Aspects of protection and risk, however, manifest themselves in a variety of environmental layers. These layers range from the home, to the neighborhood, the community, the metropolitan area, region, nation, and globe. Place is a multidimensional, hierarchical phenomenon. All human action takes place in space, but this space is more than a physical container; it is a social and cultural phenomenon as well. Barker (1967) portrays places as "behavior settings." A behavior setting is bounded in space and time and possesses a structure that interrelates physical, social, and cultural properties in a particular way so that certain patterns of behavior are likely to be elicited. Place involves far more than a physical setting. While a place's character is a function of physical qualities, it is also a product of risks and opportunities, the nature of the social organization attached to the locale, its political, social, and economic relationships with other places, the psychosocial characteristics of the individuals occupying the space, and the local cultural milieu. We learn to act in specific ways in certain places; we don't genuflect in bars or drink beer or eat popcorn in churches. Hence, our actions in various places are conditioned by a number of factors, all of which may operate on the individual to affect not only their behavior, but also their health. This relationship between place and health has not been adequately explored. Its importance, however, is undeniable. The complexity of this relationship is equally indisputable. Places are more than spaces. They are both real geographic units with physical, social, and cultural properties as well as personally defined places. Both aspects of place matter for health.

A Framework for the Book

As our discussion suggests, residential areas are more than a simple reflection of the existing system of stratification. Place, and the process of segregation that creates it, actually plays a role in the health and well-being of its occupants. The purpose of this book is to understand that role. In doing this, we explore the nature of residential space, with a primary focus on the inner city and the impact this space has on individual and social life. At the same time, we review existing social science theories of health and suggest how they might be incorporated into a broader understanding of the ecology of health and its implications for understanding the "urban health penalty."

The Birmingham case study, introduced at the beginning of this chapter, represents more than an isolated event. It is evidence of a recurring theme in American public health that reminds us of the power of place. While the Village Creek Dursban spill received considerable media attention, it is merely one episode in a more complicated daily drama that is reproduced across many American inner-city areas. Over the past several decades, poverty has become a distinctly urban problem with growing numbers of very poor minority neighborhoods bearing the burden of the "risk society." Throughout the book we link specific aspects of this trend with broader themes of place and health contained in the chapters.

Chapters 2 and 3 discuss general issues related to human territory and the organization of residential space. Chapter 2 addresses the question of territorial behavior in humans. In what sense are humans ecological actors? Since all human thought and action takes place in physical and social contexts, how do the socially ordered spaces in which we reside affect human thought and action? In what sense are there similarities with other species? Do humans have basic spatial needs? If we are territorial creatures, what does the absence of human territory mean for people who find themselves spatially dispossessed?

Chapter 3 introduces the reader to the importance of space for everyday urban life, exploring both micro and macro environments. It begins with a discussion of how various features of the built environment shape our experiences. Winston Churchill observed that once we have built our buildings they begin to shape us. What features of architectured spaces affect us, and how does the design of residential space relate to the nature of individuals contained within it? Are there such things as "healthy" and "unhealthy" buildings, and if so, what features distinguish them from one another?

Considering the macro environment, what features of the city differentiate it from other residential areas? We detail these basic dimensions of the urban residential space, which include segregation, density, size, and opportunity. In addition, we show how the social sciences have developed formal ecological models of the urban context that describe its basic structure and form, and the differential health resources made available to different subgroups within the city. Finally, this chapter also examines how the urban structure influences choice and action for the average resident.

Chapter 4 provides an overview of the four major social science models of health: health beliefs, health lifestyles, risk and protective factors, and psychosocial resources. These models represent current understanding of the possible social influences on health. While each model has the potential to provide insight into the role of context on health outcomes, up to this point that exploration has not taken place. To detail the consequences of spatial structure for physical and mental health, we explore the following: 1) the relationship between place variables and various aspects of culture, including health beliefs and health lifestyles; 2) the relationship between place and an individual's access to health resources; 3) the impact of place on risky circumstances; and 4) a place's influence on social networks and supports and an individual's access to protection against risk. In so doing, we develop a synthetic model of the ecology of health. This chapter provides the springboard for developing a place-based understanding of the potential health disparities that exist among persons living in highly developed urbanized societies. In addition, it points to a set of programs which may be used to redress these inequities.

Chapters 5 through 7 take the synthetic theory developed in the previous chapter and apply it to specific health-related issues for inner city populations. Beginning with Chapter 5, we review an extensive empirical literature that shows how the city can be characterized as a mosaic of risks and protection. Typically, the risk and protective factors model has been used to explain health-compromising behaviors among adolescents; here we explore its applicability to a variety of other subpopulations. Chapter 5 begins with a discussion of the physical and sociocultural aspects of risk and their consequences for urban residents. In addition, we consider the role of informal networks and formal services in providing a layer of protection, particularly for those residents who lack the full range of resources available to the average citizen. Specific physical and mental health outcomes are inventoried as consequences of the risk-laden circumstances present in the inner city. This inventory of health outcomes is applied to a set of special at-risk populations in the next two chapters.

Chapter 6 examines the needs and risks of the socially disadvantaged. It begins with an exploration of the work of Wilkinson (1996) on the role that social inequality plays in the general health and well-being of populations in highly developed societies. Wilkinson shows that the least healthy developed societies are those with the widest gaps between the advantaged and disadvantaged, and those with the greatest sociocultural separations between groups. To show how this relationship plays out in the residential areas of American society, we look at two special populations—the homeless and racial and ethnic minorities. The homeless are a particularly important population to consider when studying the ecology of health. They are by definition persons without place. The absence of place, and more particularly control over residential space, have specific physical and mental health consequences. In addition, we look at the so-called underclass from various theoretical perspectives, showing how segregation intensifies their disadvantaged status, and then showing the role that inner-city areas play in promoting specific health outcomes related to health beliefs, lifestyles, and risks and protections.

In Chapter 7, age-related at-risk populations are identified at the two extremes of the life cycle—the young and the old. We first describe the characteristics of the young and the old as ecological actors, suggesting the significance these characteristics have for an ecology of health. Both groups find their access to places somewhat constrained by their location in the age stratification system. The discussion of youth focuses on the impact that growing up in the inner city has on the intellectual, psychological, and social development of the child, and the particular physical and mental health challenges associated with the child's residence in the inner city. We explore the qualities of the individual and the social network necessary for resilience in such a challenging environment.

For the elderly, place is imbued with great meaning, so that social psychological factors such as place memories, perceived risk and fear, neighborhood satisfaction, and mental maps can play an important role in the significance of place for healthy aging. The impact of age segregation on health is a particular focus. Segregation by age in urban areas structures risk and protection and shapes the role these two factors play in the health of place-bound elders.

Chapter 8 concludes by proposing an ecological strategy for health promotion in the inner city. We begin by suggesting that the literature on context-based health effects could leave readers with a misunderstanding of the most appropriate health promotion policy. This literature routinely concludes that while there is a contextual effect on health, individual-level effects, in the form of health beliefs, risk-taking behaviors, genetic predisposition, and so on, are considerably stronger. Although these conclusions are accurate, they have the potential of misdirecting health policy. The fact that individual-level effects are stronger by no means implies that individual-based strategies are the most effective ways to promote health and deliver services in the urban area. Well-designed place-based approaches to health can serve the dual purpose of promoting healthy places, while at the same time efficiently delivering information and services to high-risk individuals.

We believe that a place-based approach to health is a promising perspective from which to plan the healthy society—a stated goal in the federal government's strategic health plan for the new millennium (U.S. Department of Health and Human Services 1992). Without a comprehensive place-based strategy to address the health needs of the at-risk, underserved, and unprotected in the urban core, America will continue to be a society plagued by the contradiction of great wealth and mediocre health.

In this final chapter, we review two types of strategies for addressing place-based problems—removal strategies and community development strategies. We conclude that comprehensive community-based approaches to health are likely to be most successful, and we urge that they be local efforts based on the federal model of the demonstration research and evaluation programs. These community-oriented strategies should invite significant local participation and continue in the development of programs that identify and address the special risks and hazards facing residents.

2

Humans as Spatial Animals

Good fences make good neighbors.

ROBERT FROST

Human existence is about living in the space we fill. Human existence is about granting and denying the same sort of space to others around us.

PETER PETSCHAUER

residents along Village Creek are conscious of the threat posed to their health and well-being by living there, yet this dangerous place is home and thus has deep significance for them. Perhaps no single inhabitant of the Village Creek area was better known than the acclaimed African-American folk artist Lonnie Holley, whose works have been displayed at the White House, the Smithsonian, and numerous art galleries and museums. The saga of Holley's struggle to retain his residence is a strong reminder of the meaning of place. Holley lived for 18 years with his wife and children on a quarter-acre tract along Village Creek, near the

Birmingham airport. During that time he created an "art environment," taking found objects, assembling them into works of art, and then integrating them into the landscape. To some observers his land resembled a junkyard more than it did a home or studio. For Holley the link between art, territory, and family heritage involved a deep expression of personal identity—a view familiar to sociobiologists and human ethologists who see a profound link between territory and human nature (Eibl-Eibesfeldt 1989; Wilson 1975).

His rights to this heritage were challenged several years ago when the Birmingham International Airport Authority decided to expand airport runways on land adjacent to Village Creek. After a long legal battle Holley was forced to move. With the process played out in the public, the artist was able to demonstrate the significance of place as a reflection of his personal heritage and identity. He endured threats from local officials who not only attempted to seize his property but publicly encouraged poachers to take any "salvageable material" they found on his land. All the while, Holley fought back by explaining the value of his property in human and personal terms to anyone who would listen. Holley was eventually forced to relocate, but in the process people in the Birmingham area were reminded of the deep personal significance of place for humans. As compensation for the loss of his land the Airport Authority eventually agreed to pay Holley $165,000 for property that had been originally assessed at $14,000.

His new home in a rural area outside of Birmingham is an attractive, eight-bedroom, columned house surrounded by fields of cotton. Planes no longer roar overhead as they did at his old place, and his family has more room. By all appearances Holley made out well in his territorial dispute with the Airport Authority. Yet when asked how he felt about the settlement Holley remarked, "I won't say good, but positive. Things down here is quite different than the way they were. I've got to turn everything around completely in my mind to make it work. It's hard to get adjusted. . . . The other place—I knew the people in the neighborhood. Here I'm like a stranger" (Rochell 1998:M8).

The Meaning of Place

The Lonnie Holley story is one of many that could be told reflecting the deeply ingrained attachment people have with place. Yet while place has great personal and social meaning for individuals, its relevance is sometimes lost in contemporary social and behavioral science. Rather than representing a focus of interest, the physical environment is far too often treated as a minor background variable in contemporary theory and research. Even in public health, where environments historically have been considered important potential causes for illness, current multi-causal epidemiological models of disease have shifted focus away from the environment. This newer approach attributes health risks to the characteristics of individuals rather than to environmental factors, and focuses on individual rather than population outcomes (Diez-Roux 1998). The contemporary tendency to individualize risk, however, flies in the face of a simple fact about the nature of our species—humans, like most other vertebrate species, are spatial animals.

Place is more than the stage on which social actions and experiences are played out; it is more than a matter of physical and social geography. For human beings the significance of space and place runs deep. Indeed, the link between individuals and the places they occupy is deeply tied to human biology and culture. Understanding the biological and cultural heritage that binds us psychologically, physically, and socially to place is essential to fully appreciate the connection between environment and health.

Humans, like other animals, exist in bounded spatial arenas that affect and are affected by the behavior that takes place within them. In the freshwaters of Europe, the stickleback fish carves out a small portion of the riverbed and with great feats of bubbling rage and flashes of its reddened underbelly chases off males who intrude on its space. On the plains of Uganda a species of antelope, the male kob, aggressively protects its mating territory against potential intruders. Similarly, the pages of human history are replete with bloody, periodic clashes over place. These international and national disputes, from Africa to the Middle East, from Northern Ireland to Cambodia and the former Yugoslavia, serve as constant reminders of the importance of place in everyday life. Closer to home, in many American cities, groups of youth emblazon their territory with gang symbols and graffiti and wear their colors to signify dominance over an area of the community. During the past decade, gang-related crime has plagued inner-city neighborhoods and schools. According to recent estimates there are more than 16,000 gangs, with a half-million members, committing more than 600,000 crimes each year in the United States (National Institute of Justice 1998).

The striking similarity in these territory-related behaviors across many vertebrate species has led some observers to claim that humans share an instinctive urge to claim and defend territory (Ardrey 1966; Wilson 1975). Others take exception to this idea and suggest that human territorial behavior is much more complicated and not comparable to the rest of the vertebrate world (Klopfer 1969). Whatever the answer to the question of the nature of human territorial behavior, it is undeniable that place has an important role in our everyday actions, choices, and thoughts. Space is a critical sociological and psychological force and as such affects the quality of our lives. In this chapter we examine the nature of the territory-behavior relationship in human actors. By first putting territorial behavior into a larger context, we explore spatial aspects of animal behavior and suggest how humans' possession of culture may affect their experiences of place and the nature of spatial behaviors.

Territorial Behavior in Animals

During the past 80 years, ethologists have studied the impact of space and place on a variety of animal species including humans (Archer 1992; Eibl-Eibesfeldt 1989). Some of the earliest work was Eliot Howard's classic studies of bird territories (1920). Since this initial effort, an enormous variety of territorial behaviors have been described, and the biological and social functions of these behaviors clarified. This research suggests that spatial behaviors vary widely across species, with different species occupying different types of territory for varying purposes, and using diverse mechanisms to identify and maintain such spaces. For example, among the types of territory used by different species are spaces for mating, feeding, nesting, winter roosting, and communal activity (Klopfer 1969; Nice 1941; Taylor 1988). Individuals, pairs, and communal groups may thus hold territories. They can be maintained by a variety of behaviors including direct attack (dragonflies), vocal signaling (birds, crickets, frogs), odor signatures (cats, dogs), aggressive display (deer, baboon, rhesus monkey, stickleback fish), or some combination of these actions (Eibl-Eibesfeldt 1989).

Typically the term *territoriality* is used to refer to spatial behaviors directed at the active defense of a territory. In ethology it is thus more than the habitual use of a defined area; it is "behavior characterized by recognition of, use of, and some kind of defensive reaction toward a specific area" (Buettner-Janusch 1973:553). Definitions of *territory* also include this link to defensive actions. E. O. Wilson, for example, defines territory as "an area occupied more or less exclusively by an animal or group of animals by means of repulsion through overt defense or advertisement" (Wilson 1975:256). Robert Ardrey describes it as an area that an animal or group of animals defends as an exclusive property primarily against members of their own species (1966).

When dealing with humans, however, the term has been used in a broader sense, perhaps reflecting the more complex relationship between space and behavior in humans. Here territorial behavior is defined as "habitual use of particular spatial locations" (Sundstrom and Altman 1974). Taylor (1988) uses the more distinctive term *territorial functioning* to refer to human territorial behavior. Territorial functioning is "an interlocked system of sentiments, cognitions and behaviors that are highly place specific, socially and culturally determined and maintained, and that represent a class of person-place transactions concerned with issues of setting management, maintenance legibility and expressiveness" (p. 6). He is very clear to note that territorial functioning is highly variable across different communities, although it is also essential to a community's long-term health.

Another type of spatial behavior closely linked to territoriality is *individual distance*—a critical area that surrounds the individual animal like a bubble. Violation of its bounds by another animal brings discomfort and often elicits some overt defensive reaction. Unlike territory, this space is not anchored in place, but moves with the individual. Consider the example of birds perched on a phone wire where great bickering and movement occurs until they are all spaced out rather evenly along the wire. In humans, this distance varies culturally and from one social situation to the next. Hall (1966) argues that there are four individual distance zones in American culture—intimate, personal, social, and public. Intimate social relations take place in a range from actual physical contact to about 18 inches. The behaviors occurring in this zone vary from lovemaking or physical aggression to conversations in which touching is permitted. Personal distance extends from 18 inches to four feet. It is the arena within which personal or so-called primary group relationships occur. It is the normal space for conversation at informal gatherings. Often times the closeness of the tie is reflected by the distance between the interactants. Social distance is the zone in which secondary or more businesslike relationships take place. According to Hall, this varies from 4 to 12 feet. The more impersonal the relationship, the greater the distance between parties. Highly formal ties occur in public distance, where one or more speakers are separated from an audience by large distances. These distances are likely to promote one-way communication.

While tremendous variation exists across animal species in the precise behaviors associated with territoriality and individual distance, one simple fact remains—most vertebrate species exhibit territorial behaviors (Eibl-Eibesfeldt 1989). That is, space and place are integral components of animal behavior. Such behaviors evolved because they provided advantages to the species performing them. In this sense, vertebrates are literally spatial creatures by nature. These territorial behaviors are functional and, as such, species that possess them gain evolutionary advantage. Among the advantages of territoriality are: population regulation, promotion of pair bond maintenance, reduced aggression, improved efficiency in environmental exploitation, reduction in the spread of disease, and reinforcement of the social order. We might presume, like Taylor in his concept of territorial functioning, that populations or communities who do not function territorially are in some sense disadvantaged.

Territoriality appears to encourage a more orderly world (Eibl-Eibesfeldt 1989), where the species' long-term interests are maintained. This issue of order and its origin is central to the behavioral sciences, where it is sometimes referred to as the Hobbesian problem of order, after the seventeenth-century English philosopher Thomas Hobbes. The Hobbesian problem can be summarized with the following question: Since all creatures are self-interested actors, with basic needs and drives that each strives to fulfill, how out of all that self-interest is the interest of the collective realized? In sociobiology the answer to this question lies in what E. O. Wilson (1975) refers to as the "morality of the gene." His use of this term suggests the contention that certain genetically inherited behavioral patterns impose order or morality on the natural world. One of those patterns, according to this perspective, is territoriality. Ardrey (1996) summarizes this view of territorial behavior:

We act as we do for reasons of our evolutionary past, not our cultural present, and our behavior is as much a mark of our species as is the shape of a human thighbone or the configuration of nerves in a corner of the human brain. (pp. 4–5)

Territory is . . . the chief mechanism of natural morality, something more than an open instinct, more than a superb defensive instrument—in truth, a natural mediating device between the good of the one and the good of all. (p. 73)

In the sociobiological perspective, when urban youth gangs mark and defend their turf, or next-door neighbors build fences around their property, or nations go to war over a piece of territory, they are merely reenacting age-old rituals of an innately aggressive and territorial primate. Territorial functioning in this view is "hardwired"; it is the instinct to defend one's property. Indeed, it would be extremely significant if innate spatial patterns in humans could be demonstrated. One example of its potential significance would be in the area of population density and crowding among humans. Calhoun's famous work with rats (1962, 1966) is often cited, with its implied parallels to urban settings. He noted that in the wild, rat populations stabilize at relatively low levels because territoriality reduces breeding densities. When high densities were introduced to controlled laboratory settings, abnormal behavior patterns emerged, including sexual impotence, cannibalism, violence, autism, erratic care of the young, and unexplained fatalities. Crowding violated innate territorial needs, creating a condition of increasing social and psychological disorganization (the "behavioral sink" phenomenon).

A careful review of the ethological literature, however, suggests that spatial behaviors are not as clear-cut as Calhoun's rat experiments initially indicated (LaGory and Pipkin 1981). First of all, each species, and even each strain of laboratory animals, responds differently to density. Some strains of rats, for example, do not develop the behavioral sink. In addition, the pathological reaction of mice and rats to crowding may actually be a function of population size rather than density. Work since Calhoun shows that the amount of space available in the cage per animal is less important for behavior than the size of the caged population. Increased adrenal activity, a physiological indicator of stress, results primarily from reacting to a large number of animals. That is, the behavioral sink is primarily a function of increased social stimulation, rather than crowding and territorial needs.

Not only is the relevance of Calhoun's work to human spatial behavior questionable, but the more basic premise that territorial behavior in humans is genetically based (or species-specific) is not supported. While humans display territorial behavior, there is no convincing evidence that these behaviors are innate in humans. Humans are by definition cultural animals; culture conditions the human experience of place. As such, it is not likely that a species-specific pattern of behavior linked to territory can be identified; rather, it is more probable that each culture displays different responses to the same behavioral stimuli. A more sophisticated view of the origins of territoriality is expressed in the writings of the human ethologist Eibl-Eibesfeldt, who argues that all human groups occupy territories and demarcate themselves territorially, but in very different ways. While territoriality is a "phylogenetically acquired trait," it manifests itself "in diverse cultural forms dependent upon specific ecological and historical conditions" (Eibl-Eibesfeldt 1989). Thus, it is both genetically and culturally transmitted. The significance of this fact for territorial diversity and the environment-behavior relationship is explored in the rest of this chapter.

Territorial Diversity in Humans

To say that humans are cultural is to assume that our response to spatial stimuli differs from that of other animals. Human relationships with the environment are mediated by symbols and, above all, by language. While other species may be capable of learning language, no species uses language like humans. All of our experiences are interpreted with a socially learned symbol system, and all of our interactions involve symbolic exchange. As W. I. Thomas notes, "If men define situations as real they are real in their consequences" (Volkart 1951:81). That is to say, it is the meanings we attribute to the situation that affect our responses to it, rather than the objective circumstances of the situation itself. The effect of the learned symbol system (culture) on our spatial behavior is threefold: 1) it affects what we experience; 2) it assigns values and preferences to the things we experience; and 3) it creates greater variability in territorial behaviors.

Regarding the effect of culture on experience, we tend to perceive only those aspects of place that we are culturally conditioned to see. Culture acts as a filter, letting through only selected elements of the more complex environment. Language, for example, codes experience into unique meaning categories. The Sapir-Whorf hypothesis suggests that language essentially determines reality for us (Newman 1997). This can affect our understanding of space. The Zulu of South Africa, for example, have no words for squares or rectangles. Their doors, windows, houses and villages are round (Ittelson et al. 1974). Research suggests that they also lack the linear perspective and sense of perpendicularity which others acquire from early childhood (LaGory and Pipkin 1981). Seeing is essentially learned. Colin Turnbull's (1961) account of the "forest people," a group of African Pygmies, provides another example of this. Turnbull took a group of Pygmies out of the dense forest they occupied to visit one of the nearby plains for the first time. When they arrived on the plain, herds of buffalo were grazing far in the distance. One of the Pygmies asked Turnbull, "What insects are these?" and refused to believe that they were buffalo. Pygmy culture provided no understanding of the principle of perspective.

Besides shaping our experiences, culture also influences our evaluation of these experiences by assigning relative values to spatial encounters. For example, individual distance is highly variable from one culture to another. What might be seen as an invasion of an individual's personal space in one culture could be the distance of everyday interaction in another. What would be considered crowding in one may be a comfortable gathering in another. Edward Hall (1966) notes the potential for conflict when persons of different cultures occupy the same social space:

> As I waited in the deserted lobby, a stranger walked up to me where I was sitting and stood close enough so that I could not only easily touch him, but I could hear him breathing. . . . If the lobby had been crowded with people I would have understood his behavior, but in an empty lobby his presence made me exceedingly uncomfortable. (p. 151)

How people feel about their spatial arrangements and the places they occupy matters greatly for their spatial behavior. As Taylor (1988) notes, "How people feel about a location is often reflected in how they act there" (p. 81).

Culture's impact on the experience and evaluation of place suggests that territorial functioning will be highly variable. This is particularly evident in density patterns and concepts of territory. As seen in Table 2.1, density patterns in societies tend to be linearly related to the level of cultural development.

Table 2.1

AVERAGE DENSITIES BY TYPE OF CULTURE	
Average Persons Per Square Mile	*Culture Types*
1–8	Hunting and gathering, fishing
8–26	Pastoral
26–64	Early agricultural
64–192	Agricultural
192–381	Early industrial
381+	Industrial

Source: Hawley 1950:151.

Density ceilings vary from society to society. The more advanced and extensive a society's technology, the better it can absorb large concentrations of population. This evidence suggests that cultures differ in their territorial relations.

Territorial constructs and defense also vary culturally. In hunting and gathering societies, territory was communally owned. In these societies, war was seldom waged for territorial gain and the warfare that resulted from territorial disputes was highly ritualized. It was more aggressive display than overt aggression. A concept of individually owned private property began to emerge only as food surpluses developed in agricultural societies. As this occurred, more technologically sophisticated and highly organized warfare was used to expand and defend territory. About 5,000 years after the emergence of agriculture the state developed as a new territorial unit. Through the Middle Ages and Renaissance the state was generally localized, and conflict was organized according to dynastic and feudal alliances in which the concept of nation was absent.

In the modern period, on the other hand, territorial defense is generally organized around the nation state.

This level of variability attests to the significance of culture and social structure for territorial functioning. While we are territorial by nature, the way we function within a given place and how we define that place are highly variable. Culture gives human populations a flexibility in dealing with the environment that allows some populations to significantly modify the predisposition to fixed territory (Casimir and Rao 1992). Territoriality is a highly effective coping strategy. Hence, nomadic societies, which develop more flexible territorial relationships, must also develop cultural strategies to compensate for the uncertainty and higher risk that accompanies less stable territorial patterns. Casimir and Rao (1992) revise the notion of human territoriality to accommodate the flexibility in adaptation that culture permits:

> Human territorial behaviour is a cognitive and behaviourally flexible system which aims at optimizing the individual's and hence often also a group's access to temporarily or permanently localized resources, which satisfy either basic and universal or culture-specific needs and wants, or both, while simultaneously minimizing the probability of conflicts over them. (p. 20)

That culture offers a vocabulary to interpret contexts and a valuation system, which establishes contextual preferences, is not to say, however, that the end product of the relationship between context and culture is a rigid, culturally determined behavioral repertoire. Indeed, as Casimir and Rao note, culture promotes flexibility. Territorial behavior varies from one culture to the next, but this variation signifies our adaptive capacity rather than our tendency to be cultural robots subjected to culturally programmed behavior. By nature we are adaptive creatures. We can and often do adapt to dysfunctional environments, but such adjustments can be at great cost to our health and well-being. Our adaptive ability often allows us to dismiss deplorable, yet changeable environments. Since we can endure even pathological contexts, we often underestimate the significance of environment for our general well-being. There are clearly healthy and unhealthy territories (neighborhoods,

buildings). While humans who live in such settings may define them as
home and may even feel comfortable there, in order to arrive at this level
of comfort they have to expend great energy and develop cultural,
social, and psychological adaptations that may have decidedly negative
consequences for their well-being.

> It requires energy to move to a new level of adaptation and it
> requires energy to stay there. Environmental factors that do
> not conform to some model value . . . are expensive to live
> with, we pay for tuning them out by using more energy or by
> being less effective in our work and play. (Wheeler 1967:4)

People who live in such settings do so at a cost to their health. If they
adapt by using more energy and effort to protect their spaces, they are
likely to experience health-threatening stresses. On the other hand, if
they adjust to the pathologies of a place by becoming indifferent to territory they contribute to a place's disorganization.

Healthy environments are congruent with the basic goals and needs of
the culture, the group, and the individual. In this sense, the setting places
certain constraints on the choices and actions of people in a given social
and cultural context. It makes some actions and choices more possible
than others, and it makes some expectations and preferences more plausible. At the same time, the relationship between environment and
behavior is indirect, with social and cultural forces mediating it. Culture
and social structure are more important in determining behaviors and
experiences than is the immediate environment. Nonetheless place does
play a significant role in our behaviors and experiences; it does more
than merely reflect structure and culture.

The Nature of the Environment-Behavior Relationship

Place and behavior are interwoven in a complex fashion. As we have just
seen, human spatial functioning cannot be captured by purely biological
models portraying territorial behavior as instinctual or genetically structured. Place is an interpreted setting. It is far more than a collection of
physical stimuli, and as such, the territorial behavior which occurs
within it is also more than a programmed response. How people feel
about a place often affects how they act there. People with strong feel-

ings about a given setting are likely to be more protective of it. Human territorial functioning thus involves person-place transactions (Taylor 1988) that are mediated by cultural expectations, as well as social interactions and ties, which take place within an area. Hence, territorial experience and the level of territorial functioning depend on the fit between the individual and the environment.

Michelson (1976) argues that this fit occurs at two levels—*mental congruence* and *experiential congruence*. If places satisfy mental congruence they accommodate the person's values, lifestyle, and expectations. That is, persons who experience mental congruence believe that a particular place or type of place accommodates their needs. For example, in the United States, there is a general belief that the suburbs are better suited for raising a family than central cities, hence persons raising families are likely to feel congruence with a suburban setting. At the same time, because places are the stages for behavior (*behavior settings*), experience to a certain extent is constrained by the physical aspects of the place, the cultural expectations about appropriate behavior within the place, and the social experiences possible there. Physical qualities of place make some behaviors and choices more possible than others, and some preferences and expectations more plausible than others. The implication of this congruence approach to territorial behavior is that if the environment is incongruent with the expectations and behaviors of the individual, it manifests itself as an environmental stressor. It also makes it likely that people will not function territorially in such a place. Incongruence diminishes the adaptive functions of territory as well as the personal significance of the territory for identity. Incongruent places do not feel like home.

In addition to Michelson's (1976) notion of the importance of congruence between place and the person's ideals and needs, Stokols (1972) also points to the importance of *environmental controllability* for person-environment fit. Certain settings make high demands on the individual, limiting his or her control over the environment. Places with such limited controllability can thwart or block place-related needs and expectations. When these needs and expectations are thwarted, the individual's health and well-being are likely to be affected.

Geographers capture the complicated nature of the human spatial experience in their distinction between space and place. Up to this point, while we have used those two words almost interchangeably, in geography each has a distinct meaning. Space typically refers to the measurable, objective aspects of geography. It is a material phenomenon, a commodity characterized by what it contains; a set of objects and locations at certain distances from one another. It has formal properties that can be described and measured in a variety of ways including economic, cartographic, geophysical, and demographic. As a wide range of theorists from Lefebvre (1974) to Relph (1976), Tuan (1977) and Logan and Molotch (1987) have noted, however, this concept of space does not capture the full complexity of the geographic experience. Space as a material commodity is an incomplete, even deceptive conception of the lived space. Indeed, space can play a more active role, structuring people's perceptions, interactions, and sense of well-being (Zukin 1991). The word *place* is used by contemporary geographers to capture this aspect of the human territorial experience.

Sense of place involves an interactive relationship between the daily experience of local spaces and a perception of one's place in the world. It is simultaneously a center of lived meaning and social position. Place is more than the sum of its parts (Eyles 1985); it is qualitatively different from space and landscape. Relph (1985) attempts to distinguish *space* from the broader, more phenomenological term *place* as follows:

> [Spaces are] part of any immediate encounter with the world, and so long as I can see I cannot help but see them no matter what my purpose. This is not so with places, for they are constructed in our memories and affections through repeated encounters and complex associations. (p. 26)

He further elaborates the distinction by locating place at the very essence of human identity and existence.

> To have roots in a place is to have a secure point from which to look out on the world, a firm grasp of one's position in the order of things, and a significant spiritual and psychological attachment to somewhere in particular. (p. 38)

Places are locations of felt value. Attachment to place is a basic human need, integral to self-identity and self-definition. For human beings, places are much more than territories that supply physical needs; they are imbued with deep personal and cultural meaning; they are holistic and multilevel. The distinction between place and space is much like the notion in urban sociology of the difference between exchange value and use value. Individual attachments to place are often so intense and signify such basic issues of identity and meaning that persons often resort to extra-market mechanisms to fight for their right to place (Logan and Molotch 1987). The measurable aspects of the space often cannot predict the intensity of response. Such is the nature of human territorial relations.

Basic Spatial Needs in Humans

Despite the complexity of our spatial relationships, and the inability to capture this complexity in purely physical terms, we can talk about specific aspects of space that are essential to human existence. Thus, we believe there are basic human spatial needs, needs whose fulfillment gives us a sense of place or rootedness in the world. By need we mean an objective universal requirement to avoid a state of illness (Casimir and Rao 1992). The most basic human needs are for a stable supply of food, water, and shelter. But are there human spatial needs that go beyond these? While culture conditions our spatial expectations and territorial behaviors, creating cultural variation, modernization and globalization have permeated world cultures. Hence, spatial expectations may be less and less diverse over time, making these needs more universal. Writings in environmental psychology support this idea (LaGory and Pipkin 1981) and suggest that basic requirements may include the need for privacy, the related requirement of personal space, the need for easy access to social interaction, and the need for safe and defensible spaces. Together these four may supply the sense of place and rootedness that Relph (1985) described as essential to human identity.

Privacy

Privacy constitutes a critical aspect of environmental control in modern cultures that supports norms of individuality and freedom. Sundstrom (1986) describes it as the "ability to control access to one's self or group." It provides a sense of self and an opportunity for self-development (Eibl-Eibesfeldt 1989; Petschauer 1997). By withdrawing from social settings, individuals have the opportunity for reflection, integration, and assimilation of information derived from earlier interactions. This information is used to prepare the self for subsequent behavior. Private places are the spaces in which people prepare for the presentation of self in "front stage" performances (Goffman 1959).

Besides self-development, privacy provides freedom and opportunities for intimacy (Westin 1967). It permits the individual to choose avoidance or engagement in group experiences, giving them the ability to elude public scrutiny and control. As such, it allows the person a sense of autonomy. Privacy also offers opportunities to maintain or attain intense personal relationships between primary group members, limiting and protecting communication, and enabling individuals to share confidential information with persons they trust. It provides a means of temporarily cutting off communication with outsiders, so that total attention can be devoted to a single relationship

Simple societies did not provide much privacy or autonomy to the individual. In these societies, which Durkheim (1951) referred to as mechanical solidarities, the collective conscience (the shared values, beliefs, and sentiments of the culture) almost completely blanketed individual ways of thinking and evaluating. It was only as societies evolved, becoming organizationally and economically more complex (*organic solidarity*), that the collective conscience weakened and independence and individuality were encouraged. As the individual shifted from being a social object to be controlled to a social unit whose rights were protected, privacy became a critical spatial construct. In the modern world, privacy develops into a basic human need; its absence in the places where individuals live and work produces stress.

Personal Space
In addition to privacy, there also are minimum distance requirements necessary for the healthy functioning of the individual and the group. Eibl-Eibesfeldt (1989) suggests that all human interactions have distance expectations whose trespass is experienced negatively. Edward Hall's (1966) work in proxemics shows, however, that optimal behavior densities vary from one social situation and subculture to the next. That is not to say that crowding has an insignificant effect on social behavior, but that its relationship to behavior and health is complex. High densities are not a sufficient condition for crowding. Crowding is not a physical phe-

nomenon but a cognitive state, wrought by the interaction between physical circumstances, cultural expectations, and the social actors coinciding in a particular space (Hinde 1987).

Most social scientists have, in the past, viewed high densities as unnatural, conflicting with the basic biological needs of the species (Freedman 1975). Simmel ([1905] 1964) was perhaps the first sociologist to address the issue of density. He argued that density produced excessive "nervous stimulation." More than 90 years of accumulated evidence suggests, however, that density has no simple association with pathology (Freedman 1975). For example, at the neighborhood level, once socioeconomic status is controlled, the relationship between neighborhood density and various forms of social pathology disappear. Choldin and associates (Choldin and Roncek 1976; Choldin 1978) found that neighborhood density had no independent effect on pathology apart from the effects of slum life, poverty, and discrimination. That is, densely populated poor neighborhoods had higher rates of illness, distress, and crime, but densely populated better-off neighborhoods did not.

On the other hand, at the household level, the impact of density on everyday life is more straightforward. High density in the home "increases opportunities for disagreement, aggression, frustration, and general dissatisfaction among household members" (Baldassare 1981; Gove, Hughes, and Galle 1979). High household density appears to be a stressor for individuals with limited control over the domestic setting. Baldassare (1981) finds that household crowding is particularly stressful to mothers, to parents living in a household where they are not the head or married to the head, and to parents of young children or adolescents. The chronic stress produced by overcrowding in the home has its greatest impact on parent-child relationships. Booth and Edwards (1976) note that in an American sample, high densities apparently increased parent's use of physical punishment. In a sample of residents of Hong Kong, one of the most crowded cities in the world, Mitchell (1971) finds that while residents in crowded housing were more likely to be unhappy and worried (general indicators of strain), they showed no specific indications of stress (such as mental illness, depression, psychosomatic symptoms). The high densities were related only to children's behavior. High densities forced children into the street and away from the surveillance of their parents, creating a potentially unhealthy environment for socialization. While no American studies have found such effects, it is certainly plausible that in overcrowded, unpleasant physical circumstances lower-income urban children spend more time outside in the streets—and hence less time under surveillance.

One way in which people can adjust to household crowding is by relying on an agreed social order to reduce the stressful effects of this negative circumstance. Research findings suggest that while this adjustment benefits some, it creates disadvantages for less powerful members of the family. Age stratification is a basic form of social order in all societies. Apparently in high-density settings this stratification is exaggerated to maintain order. People less able to control the environment, most often children and youth, experience the greatest costs of this adaptation process.

Freedman (1975) describes this phenomenon in terms of a *density-intensity hypothesis*. Crowded conditions exaggerate traditional role relationships. Using various role-playing situations in a controlled laboratory setting, he finds that gender roles are intensified in high-density settings. In a competitive setting, when crowding is high, women tend to become less competitive, while men become more so. Similarly, in a simulated jury deliberation, women give less severe sentences in the crowded jury room, while men give more severe ones. With crowding, men become more "manly" and women more "feminine." This intensification of roles can work to the disadvantage of those with limited power in the household such as children and their stay-at-home mothers (Baldassare 1981; Booth and Edwards 1976; Mitchell 1971).

In addition to the importance of social control for determining individual crowding experiences, persons with reduced physical or cognitive competence are apparently less capable of responding to the stressors present in a crowded setting. Physical or mental health conditions, or limited social or psychological resources, may reduce an individual's capacity to adapt to challenging circumstances (Hinde 1987; Lawton 1980). Such persons are *environmentally docile* (Lawton 1980), and more likely to experience pathology from a highly demanding environment such as a condition of crowding (LaGory and Fitzpatrick 1992). The docility hypothesis suggests that in areas where crowding is high, the health penalty will be particularly great for those already experiencing physical and mental health problems.

The impact of the madding crowd is highly variable. For many, density has few if any pathological consequences, yet high densities do take their toll on some segments of the population. Most notably, these tend to be the most vulnerable segments of a community or household. Those with fewer resources (limited power, or reduced physical or cognitive ability) find themselves most vulnerable to the stresses involved in an environment.

Access to Social Interaction

While too much social contact, in the form of high densities, can be dysfunctional, too little contact can be particularly harmful. Humans are naturally social, requiring contact with others (Eibl-Eibesfeldt 1989). The linkages between the individual and the group have long been seen as essential to the health of both the person and the social system. Ever since Durkheim (1951), the extent of social ties has been conceived as a critical barometer of social and moral integration, which in turn directly affects personal well-being.

More than 20 years of research demonstrates the critical role of affiliation in health and general well-being (Lin, Dean, and Ensel 1986; Link and Phelan 1995; Thoits 1995). Persons with substantial social networks have better physical health (Berkman and Breslow 1983) and lower mortality rates (Umberson 1987). In addition, social ties promote and encourage good health practices by providing health assistance in various forms as well as providing the individual with caring others who monitor one another's health and health practices (Tausig 1986a; Umberson 1987). As expected, social ties can be significant in times of physical crisis, and indeed most health care, particularly for the chronically ill, is provided informally (Brody 1985).

Social support also plays an important role in allaying depressed mood (Lin et al. 1986). Mood, in turn, is related to self-reported health symptoms (Hagglund et al. 1988); anxiety and depression seem to sensitize the individual to physical symptoms such as pain. Social support generally is linked to the well-being of the individual. It provides not only instrumental assistance to individuals in times of need, but also a sense of being loved and cared for. Even under the direst of environmental conditions, social ties are critical sources of well-being. For example, among the homeless, affiliation reduces depression and increases personal satisfaction (LaGory, Ritchey, and Fitzpatrick 1991).

One's level of social affiliation is a function of degree of access to sources of interaction. Spatial arrangements are important factors in access (Porteous 1977; Whyte 1990). Some spatial arrangements bring people together for interaction (sociofugal spaces) while others separate people (sociopetal). These qualities are products of social and physical characteristics attached to a given space. There is variation between cultures in just what constitutes an appropriate space for interaction with acquaintances. For example, in America, front areas often draw people into interaction with one another. In the suburbs, front lawns receive much attention from homeowners, and thus often serve as an arena for neighborly interaction (Whyte 1956). In older urban neighborhoods, low-rise tenements with fronts and stoops closer to the street promote a great deal of neighboring (Jacobs 1961). These behavior patterns encourage friendly conversations and friendship formation along and across the street, whereas back regions are more often used as private living area.

Besides social definitions of appropriate interaction spaces, access to social affiliation is a function of physical proximity and physical features of the spaces themselves (Porteous 1977; Whyte 1990). Festinger and associates' classic study (1950) demonstrated the impact of proximity on social networks and patterns of interaction. They asked students in 17 low-rise dormitories to identify their friends and to say whom they saw more often socially. The study concluded that: 1) friends were more likely to live in close proximity to one another; 2) friendship choices that included people from different floors were more likely between people closest to stairways; and 3) people at the bottom and top of the stairs were more likely to choose each other as friends than they were to choose people from their respective floors. Thus, features of building design as well as actual physical proximity are important aspects of friendship formation. Cooper's (1975) study of a low-income housing project (Easter Hill Village in Richmond, California) further supports the role of design and proximity in promoting social affiliations. Because homes were not individually owned, neighbor contacts tended to be enhanced by the placement of shared spaces. Casual neighboring was fostered where common spaces were traversed on the way to parking lots, play areas, laundry facilities, and so forth. In addition to promoting ties, Taylor (1988) notes that physical aspects of the neighborhood, such as vacant buildings or heavy pedestrian or vehicular traffic, can disrupt neighborhood interaction and discourage public socializing.

Just as with the designed environment, access can influence affiliation in the larger metropolitan space. In places where population densities are high, there is a wider choice of friends and acquaintances, leading to a high probability that residents will have and maintain social affiliations in the immediate area (LaGory 1993). Access is, of course, not enough to ensure affiliation. While people's chances of meeting are a function of access and design features, contact is not a sufficient condition for maintaining social ties. According to Blau and Schwartz (1984) and Gans (1967), friendships are a function of neighborhood homogeneity and the ability of the person to move about freely. Propinquity brings people together, but social similarity and commonly shared interests also keep them together (Blau 1977; LaGory 1993). In this sense, perceived social distance is more important than physical distance in promoting the formation of social bonds.

Further research has qualified this finding, suggesting the complicated nature of the relationship between distance and friendship. Athanasiou and Yoshioka (1973) note that physical distance is a critical factor promoting friendships, and that some forms of social similarity are more salient in promoting proximal relationships. For example, at a given distance, people of similar ages are more likely to associate with each other than are people of similar classes. Class, however, becomes significant when race enters into the equation. While race, like age and class, is a salient social identifier, interracial friendship formation, under conditions of high proximity, is probable when socioeconomic statuses are equal (Blau and Schwartz 1984; Deutsch and Collins 1951). That is, the racial barrier to association breaks down when people of different races but similar socioeconomic statuses live close to one another.

Safe and Defensible Spaces

Maslow (1954) argues that the need for security is very basic, ranking just below physiological needs such as hunger and thirst. Security is perhaps most critical in the individual's home, where people expect to relax and let down their defenses (Goffman 1959; Newman 1973a; Taylor 1988). Since basic needs must be filled first, it is crucial that individuals feel a modicum of safety and security in their environments if they hope to satisfy higher-order needs such as affiliation (love, group member-ship), esteem (personal satisfaction), actualization (achievement), and learning. Without such security, people are likely to become socially iso-lated and lose contact with the groups and institutions capable of satis-fying higher goals.

Unquestionably, poor neighborhoods are inherently less secure places, just as they are also places where basic needs are less likely to be met. In particular, many inner-city neighborhoods are less safe and secure than other residential places in the metropolitan area, with more street traffic, higher crime rates, more exposure to pollutants, more violence, more prob-lems with high vacancy rates and aging buildings (Palen 1997). Under such conditions, Maslow's theory (1954) suggests that insecure residen-tial environments impede the fulfillment of essential human needs such as affiliation, esteem, actualization, and cognitive development. Thus, it is possible that a destructive subculture of poverty will flourish in such places. Wilson (1996) is a strong proponent of this position:

> [The] sharp rise in violent crime among younger males has accompanied the widespread outbreak of addiction to crack-cocaine. The association is particularly strong in inner city ghetto neighborhoods plagued by joblessness and weak social organization. . . . Violent persons in the crack-cocaine marketplace have a powerful impact on the social organiza-tion of a neighborhood. Neighborhoods plagued by high lev-els of joblessness, insufficient economic opportunities and high residential mobility are unable to control the volatile drug market and the violent crimes related to it. As informal controls weaken, the social processes that regulate behavior change. As a result, the behavior and norms in the drug mar-ket are more likely to influence the action of others in the neighborhood, even those who are not involved in drug activity. (p. 21)

In his view, unlike earlier American slums described by Suttles (1968), contemporary inner-city neighborhoods are disorganized. They are dis-organized because of the high risk of violence and the lack of economic opportunity that characterize new inner-city poverty neighborhoods. This disorganization is likely to further exacerbate the already weakened ability of such areas (with limited resources and limited political influence) to respond effectively to health crises such as the Village Creek chemical spill. Disorganized neighborhoods' cries for help are often heard as angry cacophony, rather than messages of substance that merit a hearing and a serious response. Is such disorganization a result of spatial circumstances—a lack of safe and secure spaces? While this cannot be argued with certainty from the perspective of sociobiology and human ethology, unmet place needs may lead to greater difficulty in addressing environmental challenges. That is, places which concentrate high risk and limited capacity to respond to risk are more likely to require design features that promote security and defensibility.

Ironically, researchers suggest that certain physical features characteristic of inner-city neighborhoods may actually reduce defensibility rather than promote it (Cohen and Felson 1979; Newman 1973a and b; Taylor 1988; Yancey 1971). These design features include high vacancies; spaces that can't be monitored; high-rise, anonymous residential structures; absence of manageable territories promoting territorial identity (such as front or back yards, gardens, or courtyards); proximity to dangerous sites; high vehicular traffic; and unattractive architecture that symbolically stigmatizes residents (Taylor 1988).

This lack of defensibility discourages territorial functioning. Territorial functioning promotes healthier social environments.

> Small groupings of residents on street blocks, or at the sub block level, generate social forces that result in the establishment of norms. Adherence to, or deviation from these norms, as evident in territorial behavior and marking, allows group members to gauge one another's commitment to locale and potential helpfulness in times of need. They also express group solidarity. Thus . . . territorial functioning emerges from and shapes social dynamics. (Taylor 1988:197)

Places with higher levels of territorial functioning have higher neighborhood participation and stronger grassroots community organizations. Local areas with improved territorial functioning experience empowerment and improvement in health. The absence of territorial functioning, however, may actually promote a sense of rootlessness, adding to the hopelessness and lack of empowerment already present in certain areas.

Conclusion

Territorial behavior is an effective coping strategy used by many animal species to adapt to specific environmental challenges. Evidence presented in this chapter suggests that while humans display rich variety in their territorial responses, they have certain culturally and socially conditioned place-related needs and expectations. When these needs and expectations are thwarted, health and well-being is affected, since by nature and culture these needs are deeply rooted in the meaning systems and physiology of the individual.

Such place requirements are most critical, yet most likely to be challenged, in special populations with limited resources and extraordinary needs. These populations are characterized as environmentally docile— less capable of coping with challenging ecological circumstances. Thus poor African Americans living along Village Creek, with limited access to health care services and weak ties to City Hall, find themselves particularly vulnerable to an environmental catastrophe like the October 1997 Birmingham Dursban spill. The very territory that is theoretically supposed to order their world becomes a source of dramatic physical and psychological stress. Attempts to defend it from assault fail, and thus place, instead of being a home, becomes an indefensible territory where risk concentrates alongside limited and ineffective resources. Under such circumstances, residential identity and territorial functioning are threatened, further intensifying ecological vulnerability.

Perhaps the worst-case scenario of the ecologically vulnerable is that of the homeless—a spatially dispossessed class in a variety of political and economic systems. What does it mean for humans to be placeless like the homeless are? A gathering body of evidence suggests grave consequences for the health and mental well-being of this group, with levels of criminal victimization, infectious disease, depression, and chronic health conditions many times higher than those of other low-income groups. We review the plight of the placeless as well as other ecologically vulnerable populations in Chapters 6 and 7.

3

The Ecology of Everyday Urban Life

We shape our buildings and afterwards our buildings shape us.

WINSTON CHURCHILL

Tell me the landscape in which you live, and I will tell you who you are.

ORTEGA Y GASSETT

he emergence of cities 5,000 years ago marked a revolutionary event in our relationship to place, providing convincing evidence of our ability to control and restructure the physical environment. Since their beginnings, cities have been centers of innovation, magnets drawing people to promising opportunities, containers of great cultural and material wealth, and seats of religious influence. Cities are, however, rife with contradiction and extremes. In addition to being the source of immense accomplishment, they also have been sites of the greatest extremes in living conditions, from luxurious palaces to squalid barrios and ghettos, from secure gated communities to crime-riddled slums. While they generated great economic growth and wealth, they also concentrated hazard in the form of pollution, noise, traffic, and infectious agents. These human-created places have been associated with terms such as "placelessness" and "homelessness," which are intended to capture person-environment relationships for segments of society. Apparently, the same city air that makes some free from the tyranny of small-town scrutiny is for others a nearly impenetrable prison (Massey 1997).

Place matters greatly in the modern metropolis. Residents along Village Creek know too well the contradictions of the urban landscape. They experienced most intensely the hazards presented by the Dursban spill, yet were least able to evoke concern from those who could help. This story dramatically captures the reality of the urban space—concentrated hazard for those least able to bear its risks, and diminished ability to respond to these hazards effectively. Ironically, those places with more diluted concentrations of the harmful chemical, the areas furthest downstream from the originating spill, were the first ones to initiate an orchestrated effort to respond to its risks. This is the essence of the ecology of health in urban spaces—concentrated hazard in areas with limited abilities for protection.

Urban contexts have the power to influence our health. Yet because we are spatial creatures who possess the ability to shape and reshape these spaces, we also have tremendous potential to influence everyday life and health. This has led some social observers to state emphatically that those who manipulate the physical environment—architects, planners, and developers—have great capacity for good or ill.

> We owe the cultural map of structural change not to novelists or literary critics, but to architects and designers. Their products, their social roles as cultural producers, and the organization of consumption in which they intervene create shifting landscapes in the most material sense. As both objects of desire and structural forms, their work bridges space and time. It also directly mediates economic power by both conforming to and structuring norms of market-driven investment, production and consumption. (Zukin 1991:39)

This chapter examines the nature of these constructed environments and the roles they play in everyday life. We explore architectured spaces, how they have changed over time, and the significance of this change on human experience. These interior spaces are particularly important territories because we spend so much time in them, yet we are only beginning to understand their impact on everyday life and health. We then examine urban macro environs, the neighborhoods, communities, and metropolitan regions in which we live with untold and unknown others. While more careful investigations have been done of these macro environs than of interior spaces, their impact on the health of residents has not been systematically explored. In this chapter the significance of these spatial structures for everyday life are described, and the unique aspects of cities that shape the urban experience are identified. Using a traditional definition of the city, we then identify dimensions of the urban space that vary from one area of the city to another, affecting the quality of life experienced there. We also discuss the role of economics and fear in promoting the varying landscape of hazard. The understanding of urban ecology developed in this chapter is used in Chapter 4 to build an ecological theory of health and health behavior.

Micro Environments

The Evolution of Residence

One of the consequences of the urbanization of societies has been the development of a marked separation between public and private spheres. The emergence of the spatial division between public and private has created new opportunities for self-consciousness and self-development (Braudel 1979; Lofland 1973; Tuan 1982). In turn, these new spatial distinctions between public and private satisfy a basic territorial need presented by modern cultures emphasizing individuality (Chapter 2). As such, modern urban persons find new places and opportunities for personal growth and development of "rootedness." In her best-selling memoir, *Under the Tuscan Sun,* Frances Mayes (1997) underscores the significance of one form of constructed space—the home as an aspect of self:

> I have just bought a house in a foreign country. . . . The house is a metaphor for the self of course, but it is totally

real. And a foreign house exaggerates all the associations houses carry. Because I had ended a long marriage that was not supposed to end and was establishing a new relationship, this house quest felt tied to whatever new identity I would manage to forge. (pp. 1, 15)

From this point, the book weaves an intriguing account of the author's reflections on the house as metaphor for the self, providing a personal tale of how a change of scenery can both renew and remake lives. It underscores the notion that we are spatial creatures who seek satisfaction of our needs in places, and who have deep personal ties to home territory. More than spatial beings, we are place-oriented creatures. Place is the immediate and intimate portion of the lived environment. It is the site or location for events, but it also can be seen as having more personal significance than being a mere context for experience. Places are locations of felt value; attachment to place is viewed as a basic human need, important for identity and connection (Eyles and Litva 1998). "To have roots in a place is to have a secure point from which to look out on the world, a firm grasp of one's position in the order of things, and a significant spiritual and psychological attachment to somewhere in particular" (Relph 1976:38). It can be understood as standing for the human interactions which occur in a location, that is, as a representation of lived experience and of the larger life biography of the individual (Fullilove 1996). This link between place and self is thought to have been accentuated with the growth of cities and changes in residential architecture (Tuan 1977, 1982).

The geographer Yi Fu Tuan (1982) suggests that since the eighteenth century in the West, an ongoing process of "interiorization" has occurred in the built environment of cities. In the ancient and medieval city public and private, exterior and interior, were mixed together in ways we would find quite confusing today. Lofland (1973) describes how we might feel in such spaces:

Too many people crowded into too small a space; too many odors, most of them offensive; too many sights, most of them vile. You can't get away from the beggars and vendors. They accost you wherever you go. You can't escape the crippled limbs, the scarred faces, the running sores. Your person seems never safe from the constant assault of pickpockets. Everything seems jumbled together. Rich and poor, health and disease, young and old, house and business, public and private. All seems disorder. All seems chaos. (p. 33)

That seeming chaos was gradually eliminated in the industrial city through the use of barriers, both real and imagined. While this process of erecting barriers and more clearly defining territories touched all aspects of city life, it is best exemplified by the history of housing.

Home spaces have deep-rooted significance for all humans. The home is a "backstage area" where people can relax social conventions and enjoy more intimate social relationships. It provides more than shelter. What a house "does supremely well is to make the character of the human world vividly present to the senses and to the mind" (Tuan 1982:52). By erecting barriers to the outside world, it shields the household from the distractions of open, undifferentiated public spaces. It affords a degree of privacy, which comes to be expected and required in modern culture. In providing privacy, it creates the possibility of a distinctively personal world, not only permitting self-development but also reflecting aspects of the self.

Imagine the tyranny of a home without rooms or privacy. American culture encourages intense self-awareness and a strong, even exaggerated belief in the power of the individual. Such values had no chance for developing in the architecture of the past, and in some homes today, it continues to be difficult to achieve because of overcrowding, or poor or older design. In these spatial circumstances the place of the individual in domestic life may be unclear. Certainly, earlier rural farmhouse architecture and the tenement and townhouse structures of cities earlier in this century did not meet these needs. In the city, heavy concentrations of multistoried dwellings, with shared-wall construction, close proximity to public sidewalks, and severe cooling difficulties made for an environment where public and private space could not be easily distinguished. The often family-constructed farmhouse had a different set of problems. While it focused and concentrated on family life, and effectively sheltered the family from the public eye, it often afforded almost no privacy. The rural home brought family together for entertainment, work, and sleep, but the floor plan of these homes made retreat from other family members difficult. It was an architecture that effectively promoted sharing at the cost of individuality and freedom.

The suburban tract house makes privacy far more accessible to many Americans. Interior spaces are functionally segregated, while exterior spaces are clearly divided into public and private areas, with back yards and front yards serving distinct functions. Public traffic is regulated by limiting through-traffic and by creating natural buffer zones. Additionally, the technology of the modern home permits greater public-space avoidance (TVs, VCRs, video games, telephones, computers, Internet access, E-mail, etc.) by making it less necessary to leave the home to satisfy needs and desires. It also creates great separation between family members themselves through personalized electronic entertainment in the form of stereos, televisions, and electronic games placed in the rooms of individuals rather than in common areas.

> The superiority of suburban living lies in this segmentation of space, which allows the individual to be alone, to explore and deepen their own sense of being. In the isolation of one's house and the privacy of one's room, it is possible to think seriously and at length. (Tuan 1982:181–82)

While increasing spatial segmentation makes for growing self-consciousness and increases personal liberty, there are two potential problems with this feature of modern residential environments. First, as Tuan suggests, this architectured liberty allows the self to turn inward, but in so doing it can also become fragmented and lose its sense of con-nectedness. A sense of self, after all, comes only with a developed sense of society (Cooley 1922). This growing fragmentation of space in neigh-borhood and home, while potentially satisfying a basic spatial need of the modern culture, can go too far. As communities and families turn more and more inward, there is the potential of losing sight of the whole. In such cases, individual tolerance of others may be threatened. Indeed, evidence suggests that the growing segmentation of urban society has promoted the growth of individualism at the expense of intergroup tolerance and public civility (Fischer 1981).

A second negative outcome of this architecture is that it is not avail-able to everyone. Most notably, persons residing in older, poorer areas of the city are likely to find privacy difficult to obtain. It is uncertain whether this situation in and of itself creates developmental problems for those residing in such households. Evidence presented in the last chapter, however, suggests that in such surroundings, children are likely to spend more time away from the home in areas less likely to be under the surveillance of responsible adults (Gove et al. 1979; Mitchell 1971). Under such circumstances, children may be exposed to high environmental risks while at the same time finding typical sources of protection (particularly within the family) less available.

The Artificially Constructed Environment

In addition to the interiorization of urban life and its impact on public and private use of space, the modern industrial period is also characterized by the growing significance of artificially constructed environments. That is, architectured spaces regulate not only social environmental experiences, but physical ones as well. As Ralph Taylor has suggested, however, "nature is a basic human need" (Gallagher 1993:20). Countering that need is the fact that almost all of our time is spent away from the natural world. Indeed, recent time-use surveys report that, on average, American adults spend a little more than an hour outside in an entire day, with the other 90 percent spent in buildings and vehicles (U.S. Environmental Protection Agency 1999; Robinson and Godbey 1997). That figure represents a significant change from the past, where more time was spent in public places and outdoors to carry out daily activities (Tuan 1982).

What are the consequences for everyday life and health of this shift to a predominantly artificial environment? Winifred Gallagher (1993) suggests that the shift to architectured settings can have great impact on our emotional and physical well-being. This impact is perhaps most pronounced in extreme environmental conditions:

> "You look around Anchorage in July, and you could be in a lot of places," says John Booker. The window of his office at the university duly frames the very picture of the idyllic American campus. . . . "If you saw how much trouble it is to maintain the population here a few months from now, however, you would understand that this is a fairly artificial environment, and the farther north you go, the more that's true.

Maintaining a business-as-usual nine-to-five attitude here in December puts us at odds with what's going on outside to an extreme degree, as well as requiring a lot of money and effort. To keep a half a million people in Alaska year round is something like operating in an outpost on the moon." (p. 40)

While advanced technologies permit us to live in even the most foreboding circumstances, research suggests that the more a population lives in conflict with what is actually happening in nature, the more cases of seasonal affective disorder (SAD) it is likely to have (Booker and Hellekson 1992). Persons with seasonal affective disorder experience clinical depression seasonally, most frequently in winter, with some cases recurring in the summer. Researchers link variations in light and temperature to the depressive symptomatology that accompanies SAD (Rosenthal 1993; Wehr and Rosenthal 1989). The most effective treatment for winter-based SAD is light therapy, in which patients are exposed daily to bright artificial light for brief periods. In many cultures, light is associated with positive qualities while darkness is associated with negative ones. The Shakers had a deep appreciation of the tie between light and well-being, painting walls white and using groups of large windows to maximize natural light. "Good and evil are typified by light and darkness. Therefore, if we bring light into a dark room, the darkness disappears, and inasmuch as a soul is filled with good, evil will disappear" (Eldress Aurelia Mace, quoted in Gallagher 1993:47). As Shaker architecture suggests, built environments can effectively regulate and supplement lighting conditions and affect mood, but how many buildings in contemporary society do this well?

Temperature can also be regulated. This regulation can be important under extreme conditions, because cold has the effect of a stimulant on behavior, while heat acts as a sedative (Gallagher 1993). When cold, we feel compelled to keep muscles moving in order to stay warm, while heat seems to urge muscles to rest. The interiorization of space use thus can reduce the behavioral consequences of extremes in temperature. But the impact of heat regulation on SAD is unclear at present. While some have argued that summer's heat may trigger mechanisms in the body that mimic symptoms of depression (extreme fatigue, lack of energy, increased need for sleep), this conclusion is controversial (Gallagher

1993; Wehr and Rosenthal 1989). Indeed, some argue that those experiencing depression in summer months may have mood slumps. Their need to escape the heat leads to light deprivation from being indoors for longer periods of time, rather than to a direct physiological response to the heat outdoors.

The interiorization of living environments appears to give a false sense of control over nature, and produces a feeling of being apart from it. Nature is somehow that which is out there. Yet while urbanization and interiorization have effectively removed nature from most of our daily experiences, the human species evolved in a natural world. Nature not only is a human need, it is diminishing in terms of its availability (Gallagher 1993).

The growing separation from the natural world is but one health-related issue wrought by interiorization. As the technology surrounding architectured spaces has expanded, new substances, and new mechanical and electronic devices have been introduced into the home. This creates the potential for new, though little understood health challenges. In recent years worries about building materials have risen, with special concern being given to the materials contained in older homes— asbestos and lead-based paints and materials. Asbestos removal became a national priority as the link between asbestos and cancer was established. Lead toxicity, while not assigned the seriousness of asbestos hazards, has become a critical public health issue. Although adults are subject to lead toxicity, children are at higher risk. The negative effects of lead poisoning include reading and learning disabilities, lowered IQ, hyperactivity, neurological deficits, kidney and heart disease, as well as speech and language handicaps. These hazards are most likely to be concentrated in older, poorer neighborhoods (Edelstein 1988; LeClere, Rogers, and Peters 1997). That concentration is precisely why a known public health problem identified in the 1960s did not begin to be addressed until much later (Harvey 1997). As Harvey notes, economic dynamics fashion a logic of injustice: "The costs of lead removal would either drive rents up or render inner city landlordism for the poor so unprofitable as to exacerbate already serious problems of housing abandonment in inner city areas" (p. 89). Defiance of this logic requires the dissemination of information as well as political action. Getting the word out effectively on the risks associated with these materials, and the testing and treatment available, will depend in part on neighborhood social networks, and the level of attachment that people have with certain places.

In recent years, great concern has arisen over new materials incorporated into renovated and newly constructed buildings. While the evidence is not substantial, many believe that a range of building materials can have a significant negative impact on health. Glues, paints, and sealants often emit harmful gases, so that the use of products and materials with high levels of volatile organic compounds can produce health problems for residents. Plywoods in cabinets and flooring often contain formaldehyde that can be released into the air, while carpeting and underpadding containing manmade fibers often release harmful gases. Canada has developed incentive programs to minimize the use of these materials in domestic construction; the United States, however, has not followed its lead.

Macro Environments: Cities as Unique Environments for Living

Just as the house presents unique opportunities and challenges for human development and health, cities are distinct contexts with their own health implications. An underlying assumption of many urban sociologists has been that cities were unique environments for living and that the city's distinctive features shaped the experience of urban residents. The most famous articulation of this perspective was Louis Wirth's 1938 article "Urbanism as a Way of Life." Wirth defined cities as large, dense, permanent settlements of socially heterogeneous individuals. He believed that these three qualities of the urban space produced an environment with greater potential for anonymity, social isolation, and impersonalization. Urban spaces had the potential for promoting pathological behaviors and unhealthy places.

While considerable research and writing following Wirth's original article provided only mixed support for his characterization of the city as a pathological environment, the sheer immensity and diversity of urban communities was believed to have real consequences for everyday life (Fischer 1975; LaGory and Pipkin 1981; Reiss 1959). City experiences were fundamentally different from suburban or rural ones in several ways:

1. *Complex patterns of interaction.* The urbanite has the possibility of initiating an enormous number of social ties given the high density of urban settlements. (Fischer 1975; Milgram 1972)

2. *Exposure to strangers.* Because of the large number of residents and their diverse characteristics, urbanites share the community with many unknown others. (Lofland 1973)

3. *Exposure to unconventional norms.* The scale and heterogeneity of urban life is also likely to foster opportunities to explore unconventional behavior patterns and ideas. (Fischer 1975)

The significant scale of urban settlements can make social life more stimulating and complicated. Stanley Milgram (1972) talks about the implications of urban complexity for everyday life, arguing that it creates the potential for a unique pattern of public behavior. Urban stimuli are potentially overwhelming, with sights, sounds, and smells coming too fast to be processed effectively by residents—as a result the potential for *stimulus overload* exists. Humans' ability to process information is physiologically limited. It follows, then, that the city resident's capacity to recognize the potentially large number of fellow urbanites is limited. The "overloaded" urbanite is unable to absorb all the information from this complex environment because either there are too many stimuli to process or because stimuli are being inputted too fast. When such overloads occur, the urban resident copes, Milgram believes, by selectively reducing stimulus inputs. This can result in a lifestyle of seeming indifference, particularly in public places where individuals may feel especially vulnerable. Coping with complexity may mean ignoring the countless unknown others who share public space.

> The blank, nearly expressionless faces of urban pedestrians provide one example of this adaptive ability. For urbanites, most of the people sharing public space with them, whether it be a subway, sidewalk or market place, are nonpersons to be maneuvered around. (LaGory and Pipkin 1981:39)

The stance of indifference may also produce a situation of *diffused responsibility* and inaction in a situation which normally would command immediate response. One often-used example of diffused responsibility is that of Kitty Genovese, a young woman who was raped and fatally stabbed outside her Kew Gardens apartment in Queens. While at least 38 people witnessed the attack, no one called police until 35 minutes after the assault began, despite the fact that many witnesses watched from the safety of their own apartments. One explanation of this pattern of non-response is that the large size characteristic of urban settings falsely reassures people they have no moral responsibility to respond to someone else's crisis because others are likely to take responsibility. In short, the scale of urban contexts, like the Kew Gardens residential complex in Queens, tends to shift responsibility from the individual to the aggregate. Darley and Latane's study of bystanders (1970) suggested that urbanites are not typically uncaring about other's troubles. However, when an incident occurs, witness behaviors appear to be a function of the size of the crowd. That is, the more witnesses, the less likely that someone will intervene. This stance of non-response is often characteristic of slums and inner city areas with heavy concentrations of poor minorities (Suttles 1968; Wilson 1996). Such evidence reinforces Wirth's view of the city as impersonal and alienating. It has been suggested, however, that these outcomes are not inevitable.

Indeed, there are circumstances in which the urban context actually serves to promote a sense of belonging, shared identity, and responsibility. Fischer (1976) argues convincingly that urban scale, instead of destroying social ties among residents, actually has the capacity to create and stimulate social bonds. He claims that large size promotes intense and varied social worlds in several ways:

1. Large communities attract migrants from a wider area than smaller communities. The wider the range of places from which migrants come, the greater the probability they will have diverse experiences and cultural backgrounds.

2. Large size produces greater structural differentiation in the form of highly specialized occupations and institutions, as well as special interest groups. Each of these special groupings has its own unique set of life experiences and interests.

3. Increased size, however, does more than simply stimulate diversity and a variety of social worlds. It provides a critical mass that actually

intensifies subcultural experiences and promotes a strong sense of community identity. This critical mass transforms what would otherwise be a small group of individuals holding steadfastly to a set of beliefs and traditions into a vital, active subculture. For a culture to survive, certain minimal numbers are necessary to support the institutions that give the group its identity. In the case of an ethnic enclave this may simply mean enough people to staff the specialty shops, churches, newspapers, and clubs that service and sustain the group.

This tendency to promote diverse, small, and even unconventional social worlds is enhanced by the city's spatial structure. Contemporary cities are segregated places, and this segregation makes unconventional behavior possible by removing the smaller community from the social controls and expectations of the larger, more traditional society and its majority population.

The city's spatial organization, with its distinct pattern of sociospatial landscapes, creates a more personal world than that envisioned by Wirth and Milgram (LaGory and Pipkin 1981). Tightly segregated local communities, places with a distinct sociocultural identity, can actually reduce the possibility of social isolation and alienation if what Taylor (1988) refers to as "territorial functioning" occurs within them. At the same time, these very settings (highly segregated and densely populated areas with high territorial functioning) may promote cultural isolation and discourage the formation of ties and identities outside the local area. The very same segregation that can be liberating for those with physical, economic, and intellectual resources can be debilitating for those with limited resources (Davis 1990; Massey and Denton 1993). That situation of high segregation and limited personal resources can create a special problem for those living in areas of concentrated poverty. Segregation places real spatial boundaries on the free flow of information and social interaction. It can actually accentuate and intensify the poverty experienced by individuals, a point we explore later in this chapter.

This structuring of diversity via segregation presents particular problems for city residents as they venture out of their private residential worlds (homes and neighborhoods) into the larger public arena. Urban public space presents its occupants with a potential crisis of knowing (Lofland 1973). To carry out our daily activity in an orderly fashion, and to feel secure in settings populated by many personally unknown others, individuals must be able to anticipate answers to two related questions: 1) What do others expect of me in this setting? and 2) What can I expect of others here? Because the urbanite has no personal knowledge of the countless others sharing public space, they rely on established rules for coding and defining the unknown persons. These rules derive from cultural stereotypes triggered by spatial and appearance-based information. How a person looks, what they are wearing, where they are located, as well as the individual's body language give cues that people use to provide information about the other's expectations, intentions, and more. Fashion becomes a key ingredient in the public behavior of metropolitan residents. Clothing colors, styles, materials, and brands, along with body markings and hairstyles, communicate volumes about the personally unknown. In addition to fashion, certain physical qualities of individuals are stigmatized (Goffman 1963) such as evident disability, disfigurement, racial differences, age, and hygiene. Taken together these become representations of the inner intentions and the personal qualities of the stranger. Hall (1966) and Lofland (1973) also note the importance of spatial cues in communicating intentions. Where persons place themselves in public space (an alley versus a square), their stance (standing, sitting, lying down), and the distance they keep from others are nonverbal communications that suggest the rules of engagement, and the expectations and intentions of others.

Besides these methods of negotiating public space, a process of privatization has occurred to some types of public spaces over the last several decades. The most notable is the privatization of concentrated retail business districts in the form of large covered malls. In these privatized spaces, access is controlled and well surveilled, providing a sense of security less available in downtowns (Davis 1990). These spaces are socially sanitized, homogenized spaces, legally capable of excluding socially stigmatized and disruptive elements. Mall shoppers won't find pathways littered with the pallets of the homeless, no beggars will accost them, no signs of political protest will be found. Because of this security, such places have drawn considerable pedestrian traffic away from traditional public districts in cities. Shopping centers now account for more than 50 percent of annual retail sales, and the number of centers has increased tenfold since the 1960s (Gottdiener 1994; Jacobs 1984). This retail restructuring, however, further accentuates the already segregated nature of urban space, since most are located in the suburbs. Metropolitan areas are characterized by divided spaces and segregated places. These divisions often make it difficult to conceptualize a singular urban place because space is multidimensional.

The Dimensions of the Urban Mosaic

The urban space is distinctive because of the sheer scale and diversity contained within it. But because of the segregation that pervades it, not everyone experiences these aspects of urbanism equally. Obviously, residents of Village Creek do not experience the same Birmingham as persons living in the metropolitan area's outlying suburbs. Indeed, while the Dursban emitted from the downtown warehouse fire flowed through both inner-city Village Creek neighborhoods and outlying suburban communities, the experiences and responses to that incident varied by place.

Social Areas

The urban area is a mosaic of distinctive places, and the characteristics of these places can play a vital role in the everyday life of residents and the community as a whole. In the next part of this chapter we explore the nature of this mosaic of places (its dimensions and geometry) and its potential impact on community and individual experiences.

One of the distinctive features of cities is their spatial structure. Space is what keeps everything from being in the same place, and in so doing, space greatly differentiates urban life. People's experiences in a metropolitan area are shaped by a variety of contextual factors or dimensions linked to spaces. As already suggested, the urban qualities of space can be characterized as scale (size and density) and diversity. These qualities of urbanness, however, vary by place. Different places in the mosaic afford different levels of scale and diversity; the diversity of places is a function of the social characteristics of its occupants and the uses to which the space is put. Research and theory in urban sociology suggest several social characteristics by which neighborhoods may be segregated in contemporary metropolitan areas (Shevky and Bell 1955; LaGory, Ward, and Juravich 1980). These dimensions include socioeconomic status, race/ethnicity, and age/family status, though each is somewhat independent of the other. These independent social dimensions of place allow for a variety of dimensional combinations, producing many unique social spaces and social experiences (e.g., high-status young White neighborhoods, high-status young African-American neighborhoods, etc.).

While there is some disagreement over the factors affecting the quality of participation in different places, social area analysis contends that the neighborhood context, composed of a unique combination of neighborhood social characteristics, creates a "climate" for interacting with neighbors (Bell and Boat 1957; Bell and Force 1962; Greer 1956, 1960; Greer and Kube 1972; Greer and Orleans 1962). In essence, the degree to which people are segregated according to these dimensions is evidence of the strength of a particular "social climate" in the neighborhood. It not only shapes the social character of a place, but also encourages distinctive patterns of local interaction.

Social climate, by affecting patterns of local association, influences the degree of community attachment—an indicator of the significance of local place in the person's everyday life. Greer's early work on social areas (1956, 1960) demonstrated clear differences in patterns of neighborhood interaction between places characterized by large numbers of households with a married couple and children (high-family-status areas), and places characterized by single-person households, or households consisting of a couple with no children (low-family-status areas). High-family-status area neighbors define close-knit local ties as a critical feature of neighborhood life; residents of these places participate actively in the local area. They interact with neighbors more, have more neighborhood friends, and participate more in local voluntary organizations. Those in low-family-status areas, on the other hand, see locations near amenities and work, and neighbors who keep to themselves, as critical ingredients of a good neighborhood. As might be expected, people in these areas are less likely to develop friendships with neighbors. They are more likely to see the neighborhood as a location, rather than a place of social attachment. Work by Bell and Boat (1957) and Greer (1956) further confirms the importance of these contextual characteristics. Social participation in the local area is a product of social context and not just the individual's personal characteristics (Fischer and Jackson 1976; Sampson 1988). For example, while certainly not all neighbors in a high-family-status area will have large families or will even be married, their participation behavior will have more in common with others in the neighborhood than their family-status equals in other types of neighborhoods (Timms 1971).

Two other characteristics of neighborhoods have been shown to affect the level of place attachment—neighborhood residential stability and the neighborhood's location in the metropolitan space. Residential stability, the average length of time residents have lived in the neighborhood, appears to be important to the number of local friendships, the degree to which people feel attachment to the local area, and the extent of participation in community activities (Sampson 1988). People who have been in a neighborhood longer are likely to have more local friendships and social supports, and these place linkages, in turn, strengthen the resident's sense of community attachment and territorial functioning. Hence, areas in transition may also create a climate of "placelessness" or rootlessness.

In addition to the social characteristics of the neighborhood, its residential stability, and social climate, Fischer and Jackson (1976) note the importance of location for neighborhood interaction. Suburban areas further from the center had higher levels of local participation. While social-area analysts look exclusively at the role of social characteristics in affecting the local experience, location has long been considered an important aspect of the social space. Local intimate ties exhibit a gradient effect. Geographers have shown that residents' potential ties are conditioned by location, with the probability of local social contact affected by the level of contact opportunities (residential densities, level of territorial functioning, extent of physical barriers to interaction, etc.). These contact opportunities vary by location (LaGory and Pipkin 1981). Although location seems to matter less than ever before in terms of defining the social networks and supports people use in their everyday lives, place still matters. For all social classes, strong ties fall off as distance away from the individual's residence increases (Fischer and Jackson 1976). Distance, however, is a particularly important issue in areas with limited transportation options.

Location Models

For many years urban ecologists devoted a great deal of attention to the structure of the urban mosaic and the location of social areas within the

metropolis. The research concluded that metropolitan areas were organized into a collection of distinctive social and economic spaces. This
segregation was multidimensional, with a predictable pattern to the
location of places in the urban space. The earliest models of the city por-
trayed urban areas as consisting of segregated residential spaces organized in distinctive zones or districts. The concentric zone model
depicted a central urban area where slums were concentrated around a
business and industrial district (Park, Burgess, and McKenzie 1925).
The quality of residential areas varied by distance from this central area
of commerce, with the status of neighborhoods increasing in successive
bands away from the center. According to this view, the deterioration of
residential areas is a direct result of expanding economic activity at the
city center. Slums emerged near prosperous business areas because land
speculators allowed residential areas to deteriorate in anticipation of
making higher profits on the land in the future as a nonresidential property. In addition, encroaching businesses increased the hazards to residents by attracting more traffic and introducing more noise and
pollution into the area. Hence, the environmental risks associated with
growth tended to accrue disproportionately in the area immediately surrounding the central business district. Later models disputed the impact
of the central business district on residential arrangements (Hoyt 1939)
and suggested that the metropolis contained multiple centers of concentrated economic activity (Harris and Ullman 1945). While these models
disagreed with the single-center view of urban development, all depicted
a situation in which poverty concentrated around areas of economic
activity associated with significant environmental hazards such as manufacturing and warehousing districts. In addition, these concentrations
of poverty seemed to serve as buffer zones between certain hazardous
areas and higher-status residential groups.

Metropolitan regions are no longer dominated by a single economic
center. Indeed, suburban rings often display heavy concentrations of
businesses, jobs, and office buildings surrounding shopping malls. These
so-called "edge cities" are the high-growth areas of the contemporary
metropolis, yet they bear little resemblance spatially to the central business districts that were the economic centers of past urban forms. They
are not characterized by a dense collection of high-rise buildings, they are
not politically organized, nor do they have clearly defined centers and

edges (Garreau 1991). Perhaps the most notable distinction, for our purposes, between the modern urban space and earlier structures, however,
is in the social and economic processes that produce concentrated
poverty in the new metropolis. Slums and deteriorating neighborhoods
are no longer a product of urban economic expansion, but of a loss of
work in the city (Wilson 1996). The inner-city areas of contemporary
American cities have experienced a steady loss of the type of work that
their residents are capable of performing. The global economy characterized by flexible production and the growth of producer services fuel the
expansion of edge cities at the expense of the urban core (Greene 1997).

While inner-city areas in industrial societies have always featured concentrated poverty, for the last several decades there has been an increase
in the concentration of African-American poverty and joblessness in the
inner city. As Wilson notes (1997), a neighborhood containing poor
employed people is a different place from one with poor and unemployed residents. This is the distinctive feature of the postmodern inner-
city area. Economists began to notice a trend in this direction as early as
the 1950s, when traditional urban manufacturing and retail activities
began to decentralize. By the next decade they were writing about the
growing mismatch between jobs and the skills present in residential
areas nearest these opportunities (Kain 1968). Kain suggested that the
levels of underemployment and unemployment in predominantly
African-American inner-city areas were growing because of this spatial
mismatch. The lower-level skills of the inner-city labor force contrasted
with the high skill levels required of job categories growing fastest in the
center city (banking, administrative, and communication-related activities). Since the 1970s, large American metropolises have experienced a
dramatic polarization of social space, with large central cities developing
dramatic concentrations of ethnic poverty and joblessness (Morenoff
and Tienda 1997). Paul Jargowsky (1997) demonstrates the pervasive
and dramatic nature of this intensifying concentration of the poor in
central-city, ethnically segregated neighborhoods. His review of census
tract data for the United States from 1970 to 1990 reveals the dimensions of this spatial polarization:

• While the number of poor in metropolitan areas grew by 37 percent
during these twenty years, the number of poor residing in high-

poverty neighborhoods (tracts with 40 percent or more of total households below the poverty line) rose by 98 percent.

- The number of poor persons living in high-poverty neighborhoods nearly doubled, from 1.9 million to 3.7 million.

- The number of high-poverty neighborhoods more than doubled, suggesting the spread of urban blight.

- Urban poverty concentration varied dramatically by race. The greatest concentrations of urban poverty were for African Americans. One out of every three African-American poor now lives in high-poverty neighborhoods, while only 6 percent of poor Whites live in highly concentrated areas of poverty.

- By 1990, half of all high-poverty neighborhoods were Black ghettos. Almost all of the growth in high-poverty neighborhoods took place in central cities.

This tendency toward the growth of high-poverty neighborhoods is significant because in such places people must deal not just with their own poverty, but with the poverty of those around them. The high degree of stress associated with personal poverty is thus magnified by a contextual effect—a situation with obvious consequences for the physical and mental health of residents. Daily life for the inner-city resident is characterized by the confluence of personal and contextual stressors associated with poverty (Smith 1988).

Although the new urban sociology downplays the distinctive nature of the metropolis's inner-city and outer-city areas, with much being made of the fact that suburbia is not a singular homogeneous place, real differences remain in the social areas of the city. The deconcentration of the metropolitan region is a reality linked directly to economic and political forces in late American capitalism (Gottdiener 1985). The shift of industrial jobs from the central city to the suburbs, to the Sunbelt, and to foreign countries has accentuated the divisions between inner city and outer city (Jargowsky 1997, Wilson 1996). The deconcentration of the metropolitan region stands in sharp contrast to the heavy concentration of inner-city poverty.

Where people live in the deconcentrated metropolitan region makes a difference in their own health and welfare. The metropolis is a highly segregated place consisting of many distinct social areas. The scale of life and the social characteristics of residents vary widely. These factors affect the social climate and ultimately the level of attachment people have to the local residential space. In turn, various places in the metropolis afford different access to resources and opportunities and different levels of exposure to hazard. Together, these differences create a mosaic of social and health experiences in the metropolitan region—a wide and very visible divide.

Capitalism and Landscapes of Hazard and Despair

The divided landscape of the contemporary city is a consequence of powerful social and economic forces. Places are social spaces transformed by users not only into areas of everyday interaction but also into commodities. That is, not only do the neighborhoods and houses of residents have intrinsic value as the home where people live and carry out their daily lives, they also have value as a commodity to be bought and sold in the real estate market. Various locations have both "use value" and "exchange value" (Lefebvre 1974; Logan and Molotch 1987). In some sense, this is one aspect of the distinction between place and space—place being a complex *phenomenon* intertwining personal, cultural, and social factors, and space being a *container* of objects and locations with measurable dimensions. Exchange value and use value, however, are not merely complementary views of the same thing; rather, they are competing ways of valuing locations. This conflict plays itself out in metropolitan areas in ways that do more than constrain the choices of friends and role models in neighborhoods. It literally shapes the urban landscape, determining the location of activities, resources, hazards, and people, and ultimately the life chances attached to residents in various segments of the urban mosaic. Its consequences can be catastrophic for some.

The link between urban space and markets is ancient, but as Logan and Molotch (1987) point out, the commodification of place in the United States represents a near-idealized version of capitalism's transformation of the urban landscape. While the early industrial period promoted urban growth and linked markets to places, as capital became more portable in the global economy the idea of place has been trivialized (Zukin 1991). The use value of place yields to its exchange value in this economy, and exchange value is determined by forces in a placeless, often unregulated global realm. The same industrial product can be produced now in a variety of places throughout the world, so the jobs involved in manufacturing these products can also be quickly shifted. As Zukin (1991) suggests, this is the basic problem confronting modern communities—capital moves, communities don't. As capital decouples from place, spaces become commodities responding to ever-shifting international economic forces. Capital shapes and controls the urban ecology. Ultimately the same forces that built an urban space can destroy it, and residents can do little about it except move.

At the heart of modern capitalism is an energy of creative destruction (Schumpeter 1961). Capitalism involves recurrent innovation, innovation which leaves in its wake a pattern of destruction in which "capital creates and destroys its own landscape" (Zukin 1991:19). Thus, in addition to referring to the metropolis as a mosaic of social worlds, we can describe it as a landscape of uneven development with enormous discrepancies in the socioeconomic conditions of the city's social areas. The structural reorganization of center-city economies touches most directly the lives of people already poor. As low-skill jobs decline dramatically with economic restructuring, economic deprivation accelerates in those areas that in the past may have been contiguous to development. This deprivation changes not only the opportunity structure in these areas, but also transforms their social climate. Places that have experienced a decline in low-skill jobs are eventually touched by higher crime rates and a general environment of violence (Shihadeh and Ousey 1998). In this sense, the undulations and rhythms natural to capitalism produce devastating ecological changes, creating the context for fear, hopelessness, and placelessness.

The link between the ecology of opportunity and the ecology of hazard is deeply entrenched in global capitalism, shaping landscapes of fear and despair. One of the best predictors of the location of toxic waste dumps in the United States is the geographical concentration of people of low income and color (Harvey 1997). Chicago's Southeast Side is a case in point. A predominantly African-American area with more than

150,000 people, it has 50 commercially owned hazardous waste land-fills and more than 100 abandoned toxic waste dumps. Not surprisingly, it also has one of the highest cancer rates in the United States (Bullard 1994).

The environmental justice movement draws direct attention to the nature of the problem. Harvey (1997) reviews the political-economic dynamics of this concentration of hazard. First, the location of toxic dumps is less costly in low-income areas and also has less impact on property values in these places. Second, a small transfer payment to cover the negative effects of location may be significant to the poor, while basically irrelevant to the better-off. This situation is particularly paradoxical because the rich are unlikely to give up an amenity at any price, and the poor, who can least endure the loss, are likely to give it up for a mere pittance. Third, the poor generally live in areas with weak political organization and hence are unable to resist the relocation of health-depriving hazards. These economic forces obviously produce environmental injustices and a vastly uneven terrain of hazard and risk in cities. Not only is the world a more hazardous place than ever before, but these dangers tend to be more spatially focused. The concentration of hazard, noted by urban ecologists since the 1920s, has increased in the last 30 years in American cities.

> The accelerating and spatially deepening uneven processes of "creative destruction" leave urban communities uprooted and displaced while propelling others on to new dizzy and commanding heights. . . . For the privileged—who are able to benefit from new technologies, new multimedia and modes of communication—movement, access and mobility have been augmented. . . . Meanwhile, there are those on the receiving end of this process—like the impoverished, the aged, the unemployed . . . —who have increasingly been imprisoned by it. (Merrifield and Swyngedouw 1997:12)

While hazard and danger have concentrated in inner-city areas, fear has concomitantly intensified in middle-class areas. This divide, and the ecology of fear that it perpetuates, are precisely what Wilkinson (1996) had in mind when he talked about unhealthy postmodern societies. Understanding the shape of this uneven landscape and the processes that underlie it is essential to understanding the patterned inequality of health. Ultimately, as Wilkinson (1996) notes, it is also essential to understanding and addressing the significant health losses that accrue to wealthy social systems with such disparities.

The dramatic spatial inequality of postmodern American cities has deep consequences for the health of all metropolitan residents. The vast spatial divide between inner and outer city courses like a polluted stream through the very heart and soul of the American metropolis. The result is an "ecology of fear" that pervades urban areas from richest to poorest (Davis 1990, 1998).

> The carefully manicured lawns of Los Angeles's Westside sprout forests of ominous little signs warning "Armed Response!" Even richer neighborhoods in the canyons and hillsides isolate themselves behind walls guarded by gun toting private police and state-of-the-art electronic surveillance. . . . In the Westlake district and the San Fernando Valley the Los Angeles Police barricade streets and seal off the poor neighborhoods as part of their "war on drugs." In Watts, developer Alexander Haagen demonstrates his strategy for recolonizing inner-city retail markets: a panopticon shopping mall surrounded by staked metal fences and a substation of the LAPD in a central surveillance tower. (1990:223)

Los Angeles is just one example of the consequences of late capitalism's landscape of creative destruction, where the defense of luxurious lifestyles in the outer regions is translated into a fortressed urban ecology where "fortified cells" of affluence are separated from "places of terror" in the inner city (Davis 1990). This is not merely a reproduction of the old ecology noted in urban sociology textbooks from the 1920s through the 1970s; it is brought about by revolutionary economic forces that ruthlessly divide society and intensify in cities the most malevolent aspects of postmodernity.

> The "Second Civil War" that began in the long hot summers of the 1960s has been institutionalized into the very structure of the urban space. The old liberal package of social control, attempting to balance repression with reform, has long been

superseded by a rhetoric of social warfare that calculates the
interests of the urban poor and the middle classes as a zero
sum game. (p. 224)

While capitalism plays a critical role in shaping the landscape of fear
and hazard in cities, the federal government has also left its imprint on
city space. Dear and Wolch (1987) argue that service-dependent inner-
city areas have arisen, in part, from the deinstitutionalization movement
in North America. Deinstitutionalization was intended to remove the
mentally disabled, physically handicapped, mentally retarded, prisoners,
and other groups from confining institutional settings and place them in
more "normal" residential settings. While well-intentioned, it actually
flooded local communities with service-dependent individuals. As institutions closed, the people discharged from them gravitated toward specific areas of the city, typically inner-city areas where they found
affordable housing. "As dependent persons migrated to those urban
locations (often from considerable distances outside the city), they
attracted more services which themselves acted as a magnet for yet more
needy persons" (Dear and Wolch 1987:4). This process further reinforced the ecology of fear and despair perpetuated by economic forces.

How Spatial Structures Affect Our Choices:
A Constrained-Choice Approach

The foregoing discussions demonstrate the importance of place for the
everyday experiences of metropolitan residents. While early urban analysts such as Wirth thought that the scale and diversity of urban life
would lead to social disorder, that has not yet happened. But a fear of
disorder does seem to have emerged at the same time that freedoms and
opportunities presented by postmodern economies have been publicly
touted. As we have already seen, Tuan (1982) argues that urbanization
itself has led to an interiorization of domestic space and growing possibilities for self-development. Expanding choice is often noted as a hall-
mark of urbanization (Baldassare 1977), yet choices in the metropolitan
area are highly constrained by spatial factors.

Ultimately, most human problem solving requires spatial problem
solving. Location is a critical factor in fulfilling needs because traversing

space requires the expenditure of resources (energy, time, money). Following this line of reasoning, the city can be seen as a gigantic resource machine in which access to resources is unequally distributed in the urban space. The city is not only a mosaic of social spaces, but also a mosaic of resource spaces. Social and economic resources occur in fixed locations, and thus are more or less accessible to some than to others depending on the distance of these locations from the individual's home. People living in certain places will have greater access to social ties, services, and products than others because of the travel costs, both real and imagined. This so-called "friction of distance" is an important aspect of space's role in the human experience. While the friction of distance has declined dramatically with transportation and communication improvements, space continues to be significant for everyday choices and actions. These constraints are both behavioral and cognitive in character. Space imposes bounds on both our access to resources and knowledge of the resources available. The mental maps people carry around with them represent the horizons of their choice field, which, in turn, are shaped by location. A person born and raised in one section of a metropolitan area, for example, is unlikely to be aware of, or prefer, residential options available in other sectors of the metropolis (Johnston 1972).

To understand how space constrains choice requires knowledge of 1) the spatial dimensions that affect local experiences, and 2) the dynamics of human decision making. Scale and diversity are two essential aspects of the urban space. Both vary greatly across the metropolitan area, impacting the place's social climate by determining the number and type of options available in a given location. The significance of these spatially structured choices for a particular place in the metropolis, and the people who live there, becomes clearer when the parameters of human decision making are considered. Choice theories typically suggest that we make decisions based on a "satisficing" rather than "optimizing" strategy (Cyert and March 1963; Simon 1957). That is, we don't search endlessly for the best option; rather, we stop when we find something that is satisfying within the parameters of our preferences and values. In essence, once satisfied, we stop looking for alternatives until we're no longer satisfied with that choice. This view of choice suggests a potentially important role for spatial arrangements in decision making. Satisficing behavior implies that moving across space requires effort and resources (time, energy, and money). Therefore, if satisfying options can be found nearby, people will make choices without seeking distant alternatives.

But choice involves more than cost considerations. Satisfaction is dependent on the options available and how they fit with our preferences. Two aspects of space, intimately tied to Wirth's notions of the city as place, affect the options available to people: 1) the number of options available in a given place (choice density) and 2) the degree to which these options have the qualities preferred by those choosing. Perhaps the most important type of options offered in a community are the social opportunities available in a place—most particularly the range of available friends. The number of available neighbors governs the number of interaction choices presented in a place. If the choice density of neighbors is high, each individual in the neighborhood will have a higher probability of finding satisfying interactions there. In effect each place has its own "carrying capacity for community ties" (Blau 1994). Sustaining these ties, however, is likely to be a function of how much persons have in common with one another. People who share a salient social identity are likely to share other things—homophily prevails in most social associations (Blau and Schwartz 1984).

The significance of homophily for patterns of local association, however, is likely to be complicated. While a homophily principle may govern social associations, its effect on local patterns of neighbor interaction may vary depending on the statuses which are homophilous. If the homophilous status signifies a great deal of integration with the larger society and great access to resources (e.g., high income and education), then dense, status-segregated neighborhoods could encourage extensive ties in the local area, but the ties are likely to be shallow and short term. On the other hand, if the status embodies need (e.g., low income, low education, minority status) then networks may be less extensive (because people have friends here out of necessity), but the ties may be deeper, involving more frequent contact and greater intensity. Work by Campbell and Lee (1992) on 81 neighborhoods in Nashville substantiates the view that level of need affects the operation of the homophily principle. If, however, a neighborhood is characterized by residents with high need and pervasive fear, social networks may be further truncated. In such places, need and fear reinforce one another, producing detachment.

Whatever the permutations, local ecology has import for community dynamics and ultimately affects the residential quality of life. The levels of choice density and social segregation vary widely across metropolitan areas, constraining social networks in some places while freeing up social ties in others and ultimately helping to shape the character of places. While some places have characteristics that promote dense and closed networks, others encourage open and wide-ranging social ties. Space matters greatly for the individual's experience, quality of life, and overall health. The spatially constrained choices of individuals accumulate and produce the neighborhood's social climate and its ability to interchange effectively with the larger metropolitan institutional structure. In turn, these two factors, *social climate* and *linkages to outside resources,* are critical determinants of a neighborhood's "viability" (Schoenberg and Rosenbaum 1980). Research has demonstrated that the spatial dimension is an essential ingredient in the persistence of African-American minority group status in the United States; the heavy concentration of Blacks in inner-city areas has created special disadvantages that intensify the disadvantages of class (Massey and Denton 1993).

Local Friendships

Table 3.1 considers the effects of spatial structure (choice density and social segregation) on the degree of intimacy within local social networks, other things being held constant. The situation of high homogeneity and wide choice noted in Cell 1 produces a pattern of communalism. In its ideal form this may produce a very cohesive social

Table 3.1

THE INTENSITY OF LOCAL NETWORKS AS AFFECTED BY SPATIAL CONSTRAINTS		
	CHOICE DENSITIES	
Segregation	*High*	*Low*
High	Communal	Sociable
Low	Cosmopolitan	Unattached

Source: LaGory 1982:73.

space, with strong social ties and dense social networks. Under conditions of high segregation and dense population, as well as significant socioeconomic constraints, highly localized intimate ties are probable because choice of local friendships is extensive, and potential to make friends of similar background and identity is high. Need intensifies this probability, with persons unable to bear the costs of transportation and communication with outside areas having an even greater likelihood of dense localized networks.

The degree to which these individualized spheres of confidants mesh together to form a strong community bond is highly variable, particularly in communities where the transient population is high. Under such circumstances, the opportunities for interaction may be high. The number of local ties, however, may be low because of limited territorial functioning and the lack of trust in an environment characterized by transience and limited personal knowledge of other neighbors. The presence of a great many strangers increases fear and distrust, which can minimize the potential of an area to produce a strong sense of community. "Fear proves itself" (Davis 1990). On the other hand, if the community is characterized by a small number of transients, then an idealized form of communalism is likely to develop. Under these conditions, the spatial characteristics described in Cell 1 can produce a vibrant local community.

Even under the more preferable circumstance of low transience, however, communal social networks present a difficulty to local inhabitants. In a communal setting, networks are so tightly knit that there is an absence of "weak ties" (friends of friends) outside the local area (Granovetter 1973; Massey 1990; Shrum and Cheek 1987). Hence, linkages to outside resources are minimized. As has been demonstrated, weak ties provide essential links to the larger political and economic resources in the metropolitan area and empower communities. These reduced connections to the local and regional power structure inhibit the influence such places can have over their own fate. Thus, even vibrant neighborhoods with strong social and cultural ties face dramatic challenges from the outside unless they have significant resources to resist such efforts.

The second cell represents spatial circumstances common in some suburban and rural fringe areas, as well as in racially segregated urban neighborhoods with high vacancy rates undergoing a period of decline. Here the local community is relatively homogeneous, but the range of intimate friends available is limited by low population densities. As a result, people have the possibility of maintaining local ties, but their ties are unlikely to be either intense (i.e., frequent or intimate) or extensive in character. As stated previously, need promotes this outcome. While residents in general are likely to participate in some neighboring, for those who can afford the costs of transportation and communication, friendships will likely be scattered in many places throughout the urban area (Fischer 1982). For wealthy neighborhoods, then, limited liability (i.e., few local obligations and strong ties) characterizes the social climate of places with Cell 2 spatial characteristics. Low-income neighborhoods, however, are likely to be disadvantaged because residents there will have limited ties to the outside (due to limited access to other areas) as well as the potential for limited local intimate ties due to choice limitations. Low-income and minority-dominated neighborhoods with these spatial qualities suffer from both limited political influence and an atmosphere of limited liability. If the neighborhood is also characterized by high transience, the social climate will exhibit even more detachment.

The circumstances described in both Cell 1 and Cell 2 of Table 3.1 suggest a situation in which those with already limited influence and resources (hypersegregated minorities) find themselves in residential contexts that exacerbate their sense of disconnectedness from the larger metropolis. While "communal" spatial conditions can promote a sense of place, residents' dense social networks potentially neutralize these benefits. Such spatial conditions intensify the already negative effects of poverty and minority status in inner-city areas by limiting the weak ties of residents. These ties are essential to accessing personal resource networks. Residents with only a few weak ties, or none at all, lack power and the ability to garner the resources to change their circumstances.

The third and fourth cells of Table 3.1 display neighborhood social patterns that evolve under conditions of low segregation. Greater variety in friendship options allows for more freedom in the formation of social networks. Homogeneity, on the other hand, enhances the stability of local friendships by increasing the probability of satisfying choices, with people from similar backgrounds and experiences having much in common. For people with limited resources, freedom of choice may be highly desirable under circumstances of high choice density (Cell 3). In cases where choice densities are high, a cosmopolitan community form is likely. Perhaps the best-known example of this is New York's Greenwich Village, but most large cities have such places where an amalgam of ethnic, racial, and socioeconomic groups share residence, usually along with a number of urban amenities. These communities exhibit moderately strong local networks, but because of the variety of social ties they are also likely to have substantial "weak ties" to other portions of the metropolitan area. This community is capable of political action, is more open to outsiders, and is likely to garner resources effectively from the larger community. It is an outward-looking community form rather than an inward-looking one. The social climate here tolerates differences. Trust in such areas is also higher. In cultures that emphasize individuality and control, this particular set of spatial conditions promotes physical and mental health (Davis 1990).

The final cell of Table 3.1 represents a situation of "detachment" not unlike Wirth's (1938) description of urbanism. In these areas, the choice of local primary ties is arithmetically constrained, and because of the differences among neighbors, they have little in common. Such places make it difficult to find and sustain local friendships. While these areas certainly promote individuality and freedom, the degree of personal control over friendships is minimal. Trust is eroded. Such places lack social identity as well as any political control over their future. Identity and control may be further exacerbated by the fact that they also tend to be areas with high rates of transience, further intensifying detachment (Sampson 1988).

Patterns of Socialization
Because spatial circumstances affect the conditions for local interaction, they also shape socialization experiences and thus the cultural climate of residential areas. A variety of research traditions emphasize the role of space in self-development and the acquisition of roles, including: criminology (Bursik 1986; Krivo and Peterson 1996; Sampson and Wilson 1995; Taylor and Covington 1988), deviance (Crane 1991), ethnic assimilation (Lieberson 1961), and status attainment (Crane 1991; Datcher 1982).

In the criminology and deviance literatures, two health-related metaphors are used to explain role acquisition—risk exposure and contagion.

Sutherland's classic theory (Sutherland and Cressey 1960) of differential association provides an idealized version of the risk exposure view. Here the likelihood of individual criminal behavior is a function of the local context and the individual's access to a diversity of roles and norms. If individuals are exposed to a predominance of deviant norms and institutions then the individual has a high likelihood of performing deviant acts. The relationship between exposure and the performance of deviant acts, however, is not linear. Crane (1991) suggests that a tipping point exists in the relationship between exposure to deviance and the likelihood of deviant behavior. In this view, a contagion effect exists when a tipping point is reached in deviance exposure, causing the levels of deviance in the area to increase at an exaggerated rate. Crane shows this effect in rates of both teenage pregnancies and high school dropouts.

These views can be set in a broader sociological context. Role theorists argue that the structure and process of human thought are affected by the social context. "Social structures differ in the extent to which they encourage or discourage . . . the use of intellectual flexibility" (Coser 1975:252). Social contexts characterized by great role diversity stimulate the development of intellectual flexibility and self-direction. If people are exposed to complex social environments, with competing expectations (role articulation), the individual is forced to evaluate and reflect upon appropriate courses of action. This situation promotes innovation (deviation from the local norms and patterns of behavior) rather than conformity. In essence, this is one of the weaknesses of strong ties suggested by Granovetter (1973a and b). In highly segregated, dense settings, peer pressure becomes intense. The communalism of Cell 1, Table 3.1, can have contagion-like effects on the behaviors of its residents. Obviously the social linkages shaped by locale have direct bearing on the behavioral repertoire available to participants. In this sense, the same forces that constrain friendship choices should also channel likely paths of behavior via learned values and norms and available role models (Wilson 1996).

Table 3.2 presents the likely consequences of various spatial contexts for socialization outcomes in neighborhoods and communities. As such, they depict another aspect of the expected relationship between space and social climate. The phrases used to describe various outcomes reflect terms used in Robert Merton's classic essay on deviance (1968). We

Table 3.2

THE LIKELY PATHS OF BEHAVIOR IN VARIOUS SPATIAL CONTEXTS

	CHOICE DENSITIES OF ROLE MODELS	
DIVERSITY OF NORM	High	Low
Low	Conformity	Ritualism
High	Innovation	Retreat

Source: LaGory 1982:75.

assume that, particularly for the young with limited mobility (no access to regular transportation), commitment to a given behavioral pattern will be affected by 1) the diversity of roles and norms present in the neighborhood (degree of segregation); 2) the extent of role models available there (choice density); and 3) the youth's awareness and exposure to norms and role models outside the local context. Of course, in modern societies, role models and behavioral repertoire are readily available from a variety of extraspatial sources—print media, radio and television—so that at least awareness and exposure to alternatives may be constant. If there is reasonable consistency of awareness, then local features should play a special role in the development of local subculture for less mobile groups (youth and elders). As youths gain access to transportation this may change somewhat, although the evidence presented earlier on social areas suggests a local effect for all age groups.

The first cell of Table 3.2 portrays a situation of high choice but limited diversity in the range of role models available. This situation, common in inner-city neighborhoods, is likely to produce high levels of conformity to the prevailing local norms. In cases where the neighborhood is riddled with illicit activity and local institutions supporting deviance, young persons learn to conform to deviant expectations. This environment promotes the presence of a pervasive local deviant subculture. Under this spatial circumstance, lifestyle orientations are relatively homogeneous, but the individual is given the illusion of some choice between role models. Here local ties are intense, but role articulation is low (i.e., limited presence of conflicting roles). Thus, both private conformity to neighborhood peer standards and limited individual autonomy are the rule.

The ritualist of Cell 2, on the other hand, may be more capable of independent action because ties are less intimate and more "sociable." While individuals are likely to experience similarly low levels of role articulation, peer choices are very limited. This situation is likely to encourage public acceptance of local norms, but individuals may be more inclined to seek role models in the public arena (media) or in other areas. In essence, pressures to conform to the local social climate are less significant than in Cell 1.

The last two cells of Table 3.2 describe spatial conditions that afford individuals greater opportunities for autonomy. The choice of role models in the cosmopolitan community are wide ranging, both in number and variety. In this case, role articulation is more plausible and friendships are less spatially confined than in Cell 1. People have connections (weak ties) to other areas. Here the individual is free to be more innovative, and community tolerance is likely to be higher than in conditions of conformity or ritualism. In this case, people may be encouraged to consider alternative lifestyles, and no single subculture is promoted. The retreatist stance is most likely when role articulation is probable but the choice of available role models is constrained. This condition is potentially alienating because individual freedom is encouraged (via role articulation) but the local area does not offer the array of social networks to exert this independence, a fact which may lead to social disorganization.

Conclusion

Both interior spaces and neighborhood places have the potential to affect individuals' lives in many ways. As we demonstrate in Chapter 4, health is in part a function of human experiences and actions. To understand the experiential and behavioral factors connected to health, we must be cognizant of the significance of place, taking into account the role that spatial structures play in constraining or expanding the choices people have and the circumstances they are exposed to. As just seen, certain spatially structured conditions (sociocultural diversity, choice densities, levels of transience, and employment opportunities) set the social climate (friendship networks, socialization experiences, and level of violence) for various neighborhoods and thus affect residents' everyday lives. Besides this social climate, there is a physical climate shaped by forces in the global economy and the local metropolitan area which impacts everyday life. Hazards are unequally concentrated, and those with the most limited resources have the greatest exposure to hazard. In the modern high-technology, high-risk society, haves and have nots are easily distinguished by their levels of risk exposure. This stratification of risks is deeply embedded in the urban landscape. That landscape, in turn, intensifies the risk experience. In the next chapter we show how these spatial structures may also work to shape people's health.

4

The Sociology of Health

*Of all the forms of inequality, injustice in health is the
most shocking and the most inhumane.*

DR. MARTIN LUTHER KING JR.

*The health of the people is really the foundation upon
which all of their happiness and all their powers as a state
depend.*

BENJAMIN DISRAELI

he story of Village Creek is not unlike those told
in countless other communities across the country that have been threatened or destroyed by
environmental hazards. Residential toxic exposure is highly disruptive
(Greenberg and Schneider 1996). The stress associated with contamination or even the threat of contamination is significant and underscores
the importance of the relationship between place and health. Beyond the
obvious physical health risks, exposed residents often report feelings of
anger, frustration, aggression, and depression, and in some cases require

hospitalization for mental or emotional illness. Many families experience disruption, financial difficulties, divorce or separation, and extended unemployment as a result of their exposure to hazards (Edelstein 1988). The community's social fabric is torn by the stress of exposure to hazards. When physical stressors coincide with the stressful circumstances of individual and contextual poverty, neighborhood detachment is likely to occur (Woldoff 1999).

What happened to residents of Village Creek was traumatic. The physical event of pesticide contamination became an acute stressor that directly affected their mental and emotional health. While people were most concerned for their physical well-being, the stress associated with the event took its toll. John Meehan, founder of the Village Creek activist group Citizens for Environmental Justice, summarized the residents' mood right after the spill:

> Residents are afraid. . . . Some children have vomited from the odor and many have had to open their doors and windows. I am very concerned about the contamination that is taking place and the long-term effects. I don't believe what the health department says. When you see dead fish in the creek, you know something is wrong.

The physical impact of environmental disasters on the residents in a variety of urban areas has been well-documented (Bullard 1990; Edelstein 1988), yet the loss of control experienced by these people in such disasters is often overlooked. Many describe feeling depression-like symptoms as their local territory and home are threatened. In addition to affecting individual health, the disaster challenged the general well-being of the local community. In an attempt to cope with a situation characterized by extreme ambiguity and mistrust, Village Creek residents struggled to understand the impact of the disaster. One resident described the situation in the following way:

> It should not have taken them so long to act. A lot of folks are feeling sick, depressed, and are worried about their homes. This spill would have been taken more seriously if it [Village Creek] would have run through a richer neighborhood that was not mostly black.

These reactions typify a community in crisis where the individual and community's quality of life is besieged. While threats to health are the immediate issue to be addressed, these threats themselves initiate an extraordinary distress process with long-term implications for community residents.

The Healthy Society

Anticipation and worry over threats to physical health are not surprising or necessarily community specific. There has been a revitalized interest in health in American society that, in part, has been motivated by an increase in chronic diseases associated with negative health behaviors (Becker and Rosenstock 1989). In addition, the recent convergence of several social phenomena, including the graying of America, technological development leading to increased risks to health, Social Security and health care reform, along with a culture that increasingly promotes self-development, has encouraged Americans to rethink their health behaviors. Expenditure patterns reveal that the U.S. population spends billions of dollars each year on fitness and health-related activities and equipment (U.S. Department of Commerce 1994). In addition, the health service industry now accounts for almost 15 percent of the gross domestic product, with billions spent on health care each year (U.S. Bureau of Census 1996). Ironically, in the midst of the "health craze" and the boom in health-related spending, general health and health care remain significant social problems for the United States. Postmodern capitalism has produced not only great wealth for some, but dramatic poverty for others. In our free market system, persons who are economically disadvantaged are also medically disadvantaged. The quantity and quality of health services are unevenly distributed geographically, and there are clear-cut disadvantages for those living in inner cities where poverty and minority status combine and are concentrated.

Besides structural barriers to good health, the quest to become the "healthy society" often has been overshadowed by our seeming tendency to overengage in health-compromising and risk-taking behaviors. Health-compromising lifestyles continue to challenge health care professionals as they struggle to find new ways to modify old behaviors. America's comparatively poor health appears to be due in part to such risk-taking behaviors as smoking, drinking, drug use, poor eating habits, sedentary lifestyles, and risky sexual practices, among others. (Blair et al. 1989; Goldstein 1992; Lee, Hsieh, and Paffenbarger 1995; Paffenbarger et al. 1993). While health-related behaviors are completely intertwined with poor health outcomes, this individualized perspective overemphasizes genetics and behavior while ignoring the critical role that social structure plays in determining health care access, as well as physical and mental well-being (Wilkinson 1996).

It is important that we appreciate and understand the complicated relationship between health, social structure, and social behavior. Attempts to disentangle the relationship have been ongoing since the days of Hippocrates. In *On Airs, Waters, and Places,* he noted that well-being was influenced by the intersection of social and environmental factors including climate, topography, quality of natural resources, and even living habits and lifestyle. Since this first "ecological" examination, scientists have struggled with identifying specific social and behavioral causes for disease.

Rooted in eighteenth-century Western European thought, modern medical practice emerged with two distinctive orientations: a "medicine of the species" and a "medicine of social spaces" (Cockerham 1998; Foucault 1973). The medicine of social spaces represented the precursor to modern-day preventive medicine. It was based on the simple notion that if a person's daily activities were regulated, health and health behaviors could be positively affected. This critical assumption represents the basis for the modern public health approach, which assumes that health and behavior are intimately connected and that improvements in health require changing people's patterns of behavior. There are numerous contemporary examples (AIDS, heart disease, cancer, cirrhosis, depression, anxiety, post-traumatic stress disorder) that illustrate how certain behaviors, conditioned by structural circumstances, can hurt an individual's physical and mental health. One of those structural circumstances is residence. Place of residence influences an individual's mental and physical well-being and is a critical sociological variable with the potential to significantly affect one's health.

In an attempt to explore the relationship between place and health, we examine four major theoretical frameworks that address the relationship between social structure, behavior, and health outcomes: health beliefs, healthy lifestyles, risk and protective factors, and psychosocial resources. We then show how these frameworks can be used to develop a comprehensive place-based theory of health. To accomplish this, the ecological theory discussed in Chapter 3 is employed to explore the linkage between ecological characteristics, health-related aspects of social structure and behavior, and the health of residential populations.

Health Beliefs

The first of the major social science theories of health is the health beliefs model (Becker 1974; Rosenstock 1966). This theory provides an attitudinal explanation for why certain individuals engage in health-protective behaviors while others do not. Developed by Public Health Service scientists during the 1950s, it was used to improve participation in programs and services, such as childhood immunizations and tuberculosis screenings (Rosenstock 1990).

The framework rests on the assumption that individuals take disease-preventive action when their behavior leads to a valued outcome, and they believe that the desirable outcome is achievable. The model has gone through a number of revisions, but the key components of the current version are shown in Figure 4.1. In an attempt to explain health-related behavior, the theory illustrates how disease-prevention behaviors occur when four conditions are present. First, individuals must believe (susceptibility) that there is some threat (disease or condition) to their overall health. Second, they also must believe that contracting a particular disease or developing a particular condition will have serious consequences. Third, they must assume that taking certain actions can reduce their susceptibility to the disease or the seriousness of the condition. Fourth, modifying factors exist (demographics, psychosocial factors, media campaigns, advice from professionals and friends, etc.) that can influence a person's perception of the disease's threat and the likelihood that he or she will take some form of preventive action (Becker 1974).

In short, the theory suggests that individual perceptions can be modified in ways that increase the chances that persons take some recommended preventive action to improve or maintain their health. The modifying influence of television and radio, reminders from physicians, newspaper or magazine articles, prior knowledge or contact with a

Figure 4.1

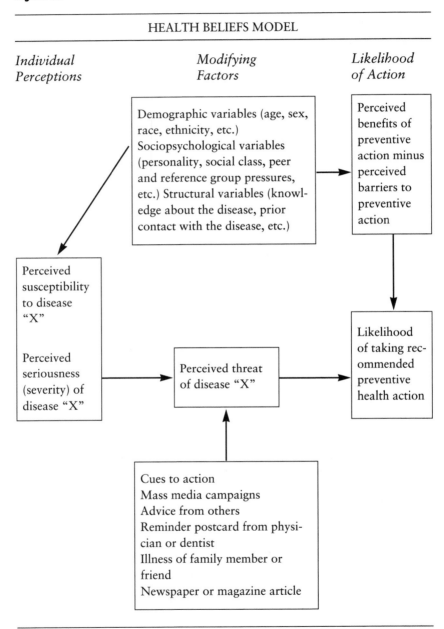

HEALTH BELIEFS MODEL

*Individual
Perceptions*

*Modifying
Factors*

*Likelihood
of Action*

Demographic variables (age, sex, race, ethnicity, etc.) Sociopsychological variables (personality, social class, peer and reference group pressures, etc.) Structural variables (knowledge about the disease, prior contact with the disease, etc.)

Perceived benefits of preventive action minus perceived barriers to preventive action

Perceived susceptibility to disease "X"

Perceived seriousness (severity) of disease "X"

Perceived threat of disease "X"

Likelihood of taking recommended preventive health action

Cues to action
Mass media campaigns
Advice from others
Reminder postcard from physician or dentist
Illness of family member or friend
Newspaper or magazine article

Source: Marshall H. Becker, ed., *The Health Belief Model and Personal Health Behavior* (San Francisco: Society for Public Health Education, Inc., 1974), p. 334.

particular disease, and peer pressure can work in combination with one another to mediate the negative expectation of individuals and their perception of disease threat. The model assumes that elements of a person's belief system can be changed in order to ensure a successful treatment or prevention outcome (Becker 1974).

Over the last two decades, the health beliefs model has been used with some success in explaining health (preventive) behavior. Applications of the theory have ranged from AIDS prevention (Brown, DiClemente, and Reynolds 1991; Montgomery et al. 1989) to compliance with laws requiring the use of seat belts (Nelson and Moffit 1988). The majority of studies indicate that the model's real merit is in identifying the role that a person's subjective health assessment plays in the decision to seek health services. Indeed, research shows that an individual's subjective opinions about his or her health is often a better predictor than an actual medical diagnosis as to whether individuals will seek treatment for a disease or condition. While not without some criticism or controversy, this micro approach demonstrates the role of attitudes and beliefs in determining health-related behaviors. It suggests that a macro-level theory of health requires consideration of the subculture's function in shaping the health of various populations.

Criticism of the model centers on the questionable ability of the factors in the model to actually predict health behavior. That is, do a person's perceptions actually have a causal effect on behavior, or do circumstances that are either out of their control or impossible to measure make the difference? Attitude-behavior approaches have often been critiqued as over-rationalizing human behavior. Some critics argue that attitudes merely offer a chance for individuals to provide after-the-fact explanations for personal habits that proceed with little rationale or calculation. In addition, critics argue that the model is difficult to quantify. Perhaps the more serious criticism, however, is that this model accounts for behavior simply by relying on attitudes and beliefs, to the exclusion of important structural or environmental factors (Bernard and Krupat 1994).

Health Lifestyles

A more recent approach to health behavior is the health lifestyles model. Lifestyles are modes of consumerism involving preferences in food, fashion, appearance, housing, work patterns, leisure, and other forms of behavior that differentiate people. Health lifestyles are defined as collective patterns of health-related behavior based on the choices made available to people according to their life chances (Cockerham and Ritchey 1997). Health lifestyles comprise nutrition and eating habits, drinking, smoking, exercise, personal hygiene, coping patterns, and other health-related patterns of behavior. Cockerham (1999) demonstrates the critical role that lifestyles play in health, showing how the broad-based decline in health in former Eastern Bloc socialist countries can be attributed to lifestyle patterns.

Life chances include age, gender, race, ethnicity, and variables rooted in a person's socioeconomic position. Life chances shape the choices that people can make; socioeconomic standing affects the individual's ability to realize their life choices. In this perspective, while people engage in at least some form of health-advancing behavior, socioeconomic position helps to determine their capacity to pursue and obtain specific health outcomes.

This model is grounded in the earlier work of Max Weber, who first proposed the idea of lifestyles in his discussion of status groups in *Economy and Society* ([1972] 1978). Weber links lifestyle to status by suggesting that the characteristics of status can be expressed in the particular lifestyles that a person chooses. Knowing that lifestyles are part of a consumption process, Weber argues that lifestyle differences between status groups are a function of their relationship to the means of consumption, rather than the means of production (Cockerham, Rütten, and Abel 1997). Thus, consumption of goods and services is a way that social differences are expressed and actually established between status groups. So, for example, a person using a health spa at an exclusive resort is a consumer with a status and social identity clearly different from a counterpart who cannot afford that type of health-improving activity or who can but chooses other activities.

As seen in Figure 4.2, Weber views life conduct (*Lebensführung*) and life chances (*Lebenschancen*) as components of a person's lifestyle (*Lebensstil*) (Abel and Cockerham 1993; Cockerham, Abel, and Lueschen 1993). Life conduct reflects the choices individuals make regarding lifestyle, which is intimately related to an individual's life chances. Life chances refer to the likelihood of achieving a particular lifestyle, based on past experiences, social status and power, and social networks. Thus, one's life chances are clearly constrained by social, political, and economic circumstances, which, in turn, affect conduct. In essence, the Weberian approach describes interplay between structure and choice, providing further elaboration of the health beliefs model.

Figure 4.2

WEBER'S LIFESTYLE COMPONENTS (HEALTH LIFESTYLES MODEL)

Stilisierung des Lebens
(Stylization of Life)

| *Lebensführung* | *Lebenschancen* |
(Life Conduct)	(Life Chances)
Risk-Taking Behavior	Gender
Values and Beliefs	Race and Ethnicity
Social Supports	Age
Social Networks	SES
	Life Circumstances and Events

Source: After Cockerham 1998:87.

While this model has great potential for contributing to a better understanding of health behaviors, a critical question raised by medical sociologists is: How does Weber's lifestyles concept translate into a healthy lifestyles framework? The work of Bourdieu (1984, 1990) bears directly on the contemporary version of the healthy lifestyles model. Bourdieu notes that while individuals choose their lifestyles, they do not do so freely. Rather, their *habitus* (a collection of objective social and economic conditions) predisposes them to make certain choices (Cockerham et al. 1997; Munch 1988). It provides an individual with a cognitive map of his or her social world, as well as behaviors appropriate for particular situations. Bourdieu (1990) contends that the human mind is socially bounded and limited by socialization, life experiences, and training. While most individuals understand their social circumstances, their perceptions are typically bounded by a social and economic reality. Habitus encourages development of a pattern of behavior and mind-set that appears reasonable to the individual, given their social and economic circumstances. Thus, what emerges is a lifestyle pattern, including a system of varying tastes (dress, food, and other forms of entertainment, including health and fitness) nested in a particular status group. Hence, social standing predisposes specific aspects of lifestyle, which may include eating, exercising, attitudes toward prevention, physical appearance, and a variety of risk-taking behaviors.

This relationship becomes most apparent when examining differences in health-improving behaviors between status groups. Martha Balshem (1991) illustrates the link between social status and lifestyle in a study of a working-class neighborhood where a public health program to reduce cancer risk failed. In this neighborhood, most residents believed that they could do nothing to improve their chances of preventing cancer; as a result, lifestyle changes were deemed futile. This finding is compatible with Bourdieu's (1990) claim that due to habitus the usual ways of behaving prevail, and extraordinary changes in behavior are unlikely to occur (Cockerham et al. 1997).

While good health is a commonly held goal, people make a variety of choices affecting lifestyle patterns and health. Such choices usually occur for very practical reasons such as not wanting to contract specific diseases, or desiring to live longer, or wanting to look and feel good, or aging gracefully. In most Western cultures, a good deal of emphasis is placed on the role of life choices in effecting good health. Even as health care becomes more structured, a menu of options bombards the health consumer as they attempt to make decisions regarding who, how, when, and where they are cared for. With this overemphasis on choice, the relationship between chances and choices is often ignored. What predetermined factors influence choices? How does place affect choices? Is place a critical aspect of habitus?

Research is beginning to establish the link between life chances and choices and their role in effecting health outcomes. Though socioeconomic status is important, it is not the only life-chance factor influencing health. In fact, certain health behaviors such as diet, exercise, smoking, and drinking patterns recently have been shown to be characteristic of particular groups of persons irrespective of their social standing (e.g., Dean 1989; Ross and Bird 1994). Beyond class, factors such as gender, place, and age also influence health behaviors. Researchers note that when controlling for socioeconomic status, men generally engage in more health-compromising behaviors than do women (Cockerham, Kunz, and Lueschen 1988; Ross and Bird 1994). The social area approach, reviewed previously in Chapter 3, suggests that places vary in social climate or style of living. The research generated from this perspective indicates that a place's social climate, independent of the individual's gender, age, and socioeconomic status, will affect the individual's style of life. No research has directly explored the impact of the social area on health behaviors. Research has been done, however, on age's implications for health lifestyles. Aging persons take better care of themselves—watching what they eat, taking more time to relax, and reducing their intake of alcohol and tobacco (Cockerham et al. 1988; Lueschen et al. 1995). The one exception is exercise, which declines with age, creating a major lifestyle change with the potential for significant impact on health.

Aspects of the healthy lifestyle viewpoint have been incorporated into the very consciousness of mainstream society. An overwhelming desire to look good and live longer and a conviction that these desires can be accomplished through wellness programs, exercise centers, corporate health retreats, and commercial products dominate a middle-class way of thinking that may be helping to set the health agenda for the twenty-first century. Unfortunately, this viewpoint often glosses over the critical role life chances play in determining lifestyles, therefore creating the impression of a dialectic between life chances and choices rather than a causal or interactive process.

Risk and Protective Factors

A third framework, originally designed to explain health-compromising behaviors (drug and alcohol use) among youth, is the risk and protective factors model. This approach combines social developmental theory (Hawkins, Catalano, and Miller 1992; Hawkins and Weis 1985; Hawkins, Catalano, Morrison et al. 1992) with social control (Hirschi 1969) and social learning theories (Bandura 1986) to explain risk-taking behaviors. Social development theory provides an important point of reference for examining the impact that prevention strategies have on negative risk-taking behavior among youth of differing ages (Hawkins and Weis 1985). Instead of conceptualizing health behavior as a function of both socially determined chances and individual choices, this distinctively public health approach concentrates on the factors that promote or discourage health-compromising behaviors. These factors are seen as complex, multilevel forces operating at both individual and contextual levels.

The salience of certain risk and protective factors varies across individuals, families, schools, and communities. Thus a multilevel prevention approach becomes critical to developing effective strategies for reducing health-compromising behavior. The systems approach to understanding health-compromising behaviors among youth is compatible with Bronfenbrenner's ecological theory (1979, 1986). Here, development is strongly influenced by family, schools, peers, and neighborhood, which, as the main "spheres of influence," act as interdependent, nested parts or systems. Each system contains an "organized collection of activities and resources that exists within definable social and physical boundaries" (Berger, McBreen, and Rifkin 1996), and each one exerts its own influence on the individual. This systems approach to development recognizes both the child's capacities to change, as well as the social environment's power to induce such change. While genetic code is important in determining cognitive, social, and psychological outcomes, the social ecology of a community creates a powerful context of influence, significantly affecting the path of development (Bronfenbrenner 1986; Garbarino et al. 1992). These ever-widening "spheres of influence" are precisely why the risk and protective factors perspective is important for developing a place-based approach to health.

As seen in Figure 4.3, the relationship between risk and health-compromising behaviors is buffered or mediated by protective factors. While the specifics of the risk and protective factors model have gone through significant theoretical revisions, the general perspective has produced a great deal of research over the past 20 years. This research has allowed generalizations to be made regarding the role of risk and protection in negative health outcomes (Fitzpatrick 1997; Fraser 1997; Hawkins 1995; Hawkins, Catalano, and Miller 1992; Mrazek and Haggerty 1994; Rolf et al. 1987). These generalizations include the following:

1. Risk factors exist in multiple domains. Risk occurs at various levels in the individual's environment. Family, school, social networks, and neighborhood all represent important elements of a multidimensional environment of risk.

Figure 4.3

THEORETICAL MODELS OF RISK AND PROTECTION

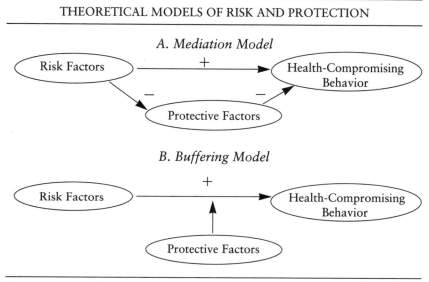

A. Mediation Model

B. Buffering Model

Source: Fitzpatrick 1977:135.

2. The more risk factors present in the environment, the greater the risk and the greater the likelihood that a negative health outcome will result. Many persons are at risk for a variety of negative health outcomes. Some, however, are exposed to such a large number that their "risk quotient" is exponentially greater than that of someone who possesses only a few risk factors. For example, all children living in poverty are at risk for poor negative health outcomes simply because they are poor, yet not all of these children follow similar health trajectories. If a child lives in poverty, has a low IQ, lives with a single parent, has no health insurance, has low self-esteem, and is constantly exposed to community violence, this child's risk level is significantly greater than that of a child who lives in poverty without any other risk factors present.

3. Common risk factors predict a diverse set of health outcomes. This finding suggests that when certain risk factors are identified and interventions prove successful, additional benefits may accrue. Thus, for example, a program that successfully reduces violence exposure and improves mental and physical health may at the same time reduce

feelings of vulnerability, while increasing school performance and social competence.

4. The effects of risk factors show some consistency across racial and ethnic groups, as well as social classes. Thus, while risk varies from group to group, the effects of risk do not, suggesting that community prevention efforts that target specific risk factors should be adaptable to a variety of subpopulations.

5. Protective factors may buffer the negative effects of exposure to risk. Research has demonstrated that certain protective factors moderate the negative consequences of exposure to risk, improving health outcomes. Protective factors are both passive and active; some actually reduce risk simply by their presence, while others change the way a person responds to risk. Armed with knowledge about these multilevel protective factors, communities have the ability to develop programs that more effectively address mechanisms that minimize or eliminate risk.

6. As is the case with risk factors, protective factors occur at multiple levels. Individual-, family-, school-, and community-level characteristics are important in helping individuals establish a "blanket of protection." Protective factors include individual characteristics such as gender, IQ, and temperament; family and school characteristics such as bonding with parents and teachers, parental supervision and interest in child's activities; and community characteristics such as healthy beliefs and well-defined standards for behavior in a community that provides support and access to resources.

The risk and protective factors framework is useful in developing comprehensive prevention programs for spatially concentrated health problems. Just as this approach to prevention has become a central element in criminal justice policy, it too represents a critical strategy for determining health policy. Developing and implementing strategies that comprehensively attend to the multidimensional physical and mental health needs of children and families is a formidable task. Unfortunately, most of the efforts have concentrated on treating the illness rather than dealing with the risks associated with the illness such as place of residence, and the socioeconomic and general life circumstances of the individual. The problems associated with this view are captured in an excerpt from a presidential address made to the American Academy of Child and Adolescent Psychiatry:

> We have developed a philosophical approach that empha-
> sizes a triage mentality rather than one of spontaneously
> helping the afflicted. We are asked to provide Band-Aid
> treatment for serious problems, and there is little thought of
> prevention. (Phillips 1985)

As suggested, a risk-based approach to prevention can be used as a comprehensive strategy to address the health problems emerging in a diverse society with significant demographic differences in morbidity and mortality. Following theories of health discussed earlier in this chapter, health lifestyles and beliefs should be included in this frame-work as aspects of risk and protection targeted for the prevention of health-compromising behavior.

Psychosocial Resources

Another framework used to explain health behavior is the psychosocial resources model. This model originates from the earlier work of stress researchers examining the relationship between life events and stress/distress among adults in the general population (Dohrenwend and Dohrenwend 1981; Holmes and Rahe 1967; Tausig 1986a and b; Thoits 1985). The model attempts to understand the intricate relationships among stressors, social and psychological resources, and the individual's mental health (Cobb 1976; Dean and Lin 1977; Ensel and Lin 1991; Lazarus and Folkman 1984; Lin et al. 1986; Mirowsky and Ross 1989; Pearlin 1989; Turner 1983; Turner, Wheaton, and Lloyd 1995; Wheaton 1983).

Stressors refer to environmental, social, or individual circumstances that give rise to stress, force people to adjust or readjust their behavior, and eventually influence the mental and/or the physical health of the individual (Thoits 1995). Pearlin (1989) suggests that two major types of stressors should be considered: *life events* and *chronic strains*. Life events are undesired, unscheduled, and uncontrollable acute events in a person's life, such as divorce, death, loss of a job, or in the case of Village Creek, an environmental accident. Extensive empirical research has shown that one or more negative events experienced up to one year in length have a negative impact on a person's mental health (Cohen and Williamson 1991; Tausig 1986a and b; Thoits 1983).

Chronic strains, on the other hand, are enduring problems or threats faced on a daily or ongoing basis. These circumstances, like life events, also have been shown to have negative effects on physical and mental health (Avison and Turner 1988; Pearlin 1989; Verbrugge 1989). Chronic strains have been linked to the social roles and places that are byproducts of the stratification system. Thus, gender, race/ethnicity, and class become particularly relevant to a discussion of the association between social position and individual health outcomes (Mirowsky and Ross 1989; Pearlin 1989).

Perhaps the most obvious example of the link between social position and health is that of income inequality (Lundberg 1993; Wilkinson 1996). Poverty represents a chronic strain with significant consequences for health. Both absolute and relative deprivation cause stress; empirical evidence shows that adverse socioeconomic circumstances have the potential for long-lasting psychological and emotional damage, particularly for children living in high-stress environments. A report of the National Commission on Children, *Beyond Rhetoric* (1991), projected what lies ahead for the nearly six million children (24 percent of all children under the age of six) growing up in families living below the poverty line. Comparisons with children not living in poverty indicate that at-risk youth are more likely to fail in school, have disciplinary problems, have low achievement scores, repeat grades, drop out of school, exhibit delinquent behavior, and experience long periods of unemployment. These same youth are likely to encounter significant physical and mental health problems.

To further illustrate the important role that socioeconomic disadvantage plays in determining health outcomes, Wilkinson (1996), using cross-national data, demonstrates that at similar levels of development, nations with greater income inequality generally have populations with poorer overall health. Hence, in those countries where inequality is modest and social cohesiveness high, life expectancy is higher. Among developed countries, it isn't that the wealthiest societies have the best health, but rather that the most egalitarian do. Societies with a narrower gap between rich and poor have a stronger community life, less family dissension, and higher levels of formal and informal social support. The resources, in turn, play an important role in promoting health.

In general, researchers conclude that these types of resources intervene in the stress process. Resources modify or at least mediate negative conditions (life events or chronic strains such as poverty) that may lead to the development of mental health problems. Thus, they are conceptualized as reactive elements in the stress process which are drawn upon as mediators or buffers against negative external stimuli (Ensel and Lin 1991).

Two major types of resources are considered critical to understanding the overall stress reduction process. *Psychological resources* are personality characteristics that enable individuals to cope with challenging circumstances. Traits such as mastery (Pearlin and Schooler 1978), self-esteem (Rosenberg 1965), and social competence (Cairns and Cairns 1994) are resources capable of moderating life stressors. *Social resources* are elements embedded within a person's social networks that serve specific instrumental and expressive needs. These networks are the supports that persons in distress rely upon, including family, friends, and neighbors. These supports are critical to an individual's ability to cope with challenging, undesirable circumstances and events.

In describing the various aspects and sources of support, Lin and colleagues (1986) point to the "perceived or actual instrumental and/or expressive provisions supplied by the community, social networks, and confiding partners" (p. 18). There are several noteworthy aspects to this particular definition. One is a clear distinction between actual and perceived support. Both types of support have received a great deal of attention in the literature, and in a majority of research, both perceived and actual supports have been shown to reduce the negative consequences of stressors on an individual's mental health (Lin et al. 1986; Thoits 1995). The definition also highlights the multiple sources of social support for individuals. These include the characteristics of an individual's formal and informal networks, as well as the nature of the community in which those networks are embedded.

Considerable empirical evidence shows that social support at all these levels plays an important role in the stress process (see Thoits 1995 for a comprehensive review of social stress research and its major findings). As suggested in Figure 4.4, the exact nature of this relationship has been a subject of some debate (Ensel and Lin 1991). The suggested roles that

Figure 4.4

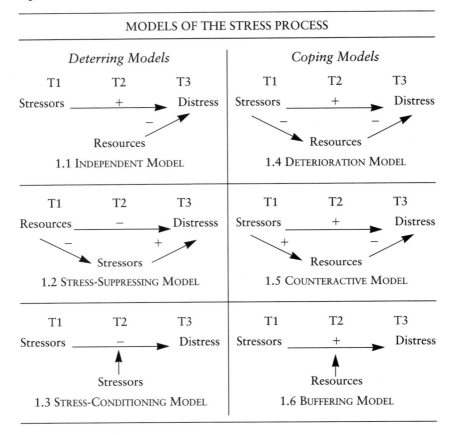

MODELS OF THE STRESS PROCESS

Deterring Models   *Coping Models*

1.1 INDEPENDENT MODEL

1.2 STRESS-SUPPRESSING MODEL

1.3 STRESS-CONDITIONING MODEL

1.4 DETERIORATION MODEL

1.5 COUNTERACTIVE MODEL

1.6 BUFFERING MODEL

Source: Ensel and Lin 1991:324.

resources play include deterrence and coping. Models proposing deterrence show resources directly reducing distress. Coping models, on the other hand, argue that stressors trigger a response from the individual's social resources that, in turn, have some impact on distress. Additionally, they point out that resources generally intervene in the relationship between stressors (events and circumstances) and levels of distress. Social science research provides the strongest support for a coping perspective (Ensel and Lin 1991; Thoits 1995). This perspective is also compatible with ideas contained in the risk and protective factors approach. Both models propose that support acts as a form of protection against the risks contained in a stress-filled environment.

Spatial Structure and Health: Theoretical Underpinnings

A review of these major health behavior theories provides several critical concepts relevant to the development of a place-based theory of health. None of these theories explicitly discuss the role of place in health, although each suggests the possibilities of such a role. Indeed, the concepts of subcultures, life chances, risk, and social resources emerge from these theories and provide crucial building blocks to be used in developing an ecological approach to health. *Subcultures,* for example, display distinctive health lifestyles, with specific beliefs, knowledge, and attitudes conditioning risk-taking behavior and health. These subcultures develop under unique spatial conditions of isolation and separation from the dominant culture. In such isolated places, deviant institutions and role models emerge that influence the health-related lifestyles of residents (Sutherland and Cressey 1960). *Life chances,* in turn, are seen as shaping the lifestyle content of shared cultures by limiting the choices available to individuals. Place of residence is a critical component of an individual's life chances. Cities are resource machines producing and distributing resources according to location; place determines access to resources and choices, influencing obtainable lifestyle options and shaping health-related practices, beliefs, and behaviors. Perhaps the most crucial determinant of life chance and access to resources and choices is the community's level of economic opportunity. Many inner-city areas are devoid of opportunity, particularly legitimate employment. This further promotes deviant lifestyles and increases risk-taking behavior. These places not only isolate residents from available resources in the larger metropolitan area, but often contain concentrated hazards. Such places present dramatically higher physical and mental health *risks* to their residents. Finally, *social resources,* similar to life chances, are spatially structured in cities. Patterns of choice density, segregation, and transiency vary dramatically across the urban landscape. Empirical evidence shows these factors are important to shaping the social networks and the quality of support found in those networks.

The remainder of this chapter attempts to integrate the four previously discussed theories into a place-based approach to health. This approach specifies the role of place in determining unevenly distributed health outcomes for an urban population. In order to do this, we use the ecological theory developed in Chapter 3 to identify key spatial variables with links to the sociological concepts of subculture, life chances, risk, and social resources. That theory outlines the relationships among the urban spatial structure, health hazards, and the choices residents make. Several important ecological factors are identified that influence the health and well-being of residents. These factors include the *presence of health hazards*; the *choice densities* characteristic of the residential space; the residential area's *segregation* in terms of socioeconomic status, race/ethnicity, and life cycle; the *degree of access* that the population has to other spaces; the *level of socioeconomic resources* contained in the space; and the degree to which the space promotes *territorial functioning* by encouraging community attachment and shared trust.

These ecological factors constrain the choices and actions of individuals in a given residential area, and these actions and choices affect the health of residents and their communities. In addition, the ecology of the area can directly affect health because of the differential risks across the urban landscape. The nature of the relationship between ecology and health is obviously complex, involving more than just the physical and psychological risks inherent in a place. The ecology of an area has an impact on the health beliefs and practices of residents, their health lifestyles, their access to various health resources, and the social network of friends and supports that help them to cope with stressful circumstances and events. Certain ecological conditions can intensify the health disadvantages of some groups, promoting the emergence of unhealthy lifestyles mired in risky and dangerous behaviors. They can concentrate persons with already limited options into areas that, because of their ecology, further restrict the lifestyle options, social supports, and health resources available to them.

In order to see how this works, it is important to review in greater detail the basic principles that underlie the four social theories of health discussed earlier in this chapter. These theories suggest that health is greatly affected by four forces: the *life chances* associated with the individual's position in the social structure; the level of exposure to *risk*; cultural factors (health beliefs and lifestyles) that create the potential for health-related *subcultures*; and the individual's access to formal and informal *support* networks. A natural question that emerges from consideration of these forces is: What bearing does ecology have on each of these and ultimately on the health of residents and their larger communities?

Risk and *life chances* are spatially structured in the urban landscape. Because housing is delivered in the marketplace, residential location is a function of a group's ability to pay for housing and transportation, as well as their ability to gain advantage and control over the market. Hence, the urban space is home to a mosaic of groups sorted and sifted according to their political and economic resources (life chances). Those with greatest resources will generally reside in areas containing low levels of risk, while those with limited resources will find access limited to undesirable areas with the greatest amount of risk. Thus the ecology of risk follows fairly straightforward patterns in which people are segregated in cities according to their abilities to gain housing. Risk, in other words, typically is segregated by those factors associated with life chances (race/ethnicity, class, and age). Communities with the greatest concentration of risk are those containing large numbers of minorities and low-income persons living in aging residential areas—the so-called low-resource populations and places of the inner city (Logan and Molotch 1987). These also happen to be groups whose lifestyle choices are constrained by their life chances or habitus.

Health-related subcultures are thus promoted by the urban ecology (LaGory 1983). Areas characterized by residents with limited life chances that are highly segregated with high friendship choice densities have spatial structures that promote the development of subcultures. Individuals in such areas develop intense social bonds and have few links outside the social area—creating what Fischer (1976, 1982) describes as a "critical mass" for subculture formation. A situation of high choice, occurring in densely populated areas, permits the critical mass that allows "what would otherwise be a small group of individuals to become a vital, active subculture" (Fischer 1976:37). For a subculture to emerge, certain minimal numbers are necessary to support the institutions that give the group a unique identity. Individuals learn cultural norms and values from role models. If the number of role models is high, but their social diversity low, then a situation of high conformity to the local subculture is likely. This conformity will be further intensified if people in the community also have limited resources to seek contacts outside the area, a condition occurring in inner-city areas where transportation is limited by low income and high rates of unemployment. Under these circumstances of limited life chances and highly concentrated social networks, conformity to the norms and values of the local area and limited individual autonomy will be the rule.

The degree to which the subculture deviates from the traditional culture will depend partially on how isolated the local group is from other communities within the metropolitan area. In "communal" areas (high choice densities, high segregation, low accessibility to other parts of the community) local social networks will be isolated. These spatial conditions promote a *deviant* subculture. Whether risky behaviors become part of this strong local subculture will depend on the presence of "illegitimate institutions" and "deviant role models" (Cloward and Ohlin 1960). These institutions and models are most likely to emerge in places where the dominant culture's goals (such as achievement, material acquisition, etc.) are difficult for the local group to attain—a situation most common in areas with limited life chances (Merton 1968). These ecological circumstances (high density, high segregation, low access, presence of illegitimate institutions, presence of deviant role models) represent the spatial conditions which nurture high probabilities of health-compromising behaviors and health beliefs. This health-compromising subculture will further exacerbate the high risks concentrated in such communities. Hence, local ecology often promotes a mosaic of distinct health challenges, combining unique subcultures with high amounts of hazard and risk. The most obvious and discussed of these subcultures are inner-city areas where the "urban health penalty" is highest.

Ecological factors also shape formal and informal social networks (*social support*), which provide the protection against stressors and other health hazards and risks. Chapter 3 demonstrates how the combination of high density, high segregation, and limited access promotes communalism. Communalism is a situation where local social ties are strong but the community is cut off from other areas because of the absence of "weak ties" to the remainder of the metropolis. Such local patterns of friendship, with dense networks that do not extend beyond the local area, make it difficult for any community to respond to threats from the outside. This may be particularly true in high-risk environments such as the inner city, where ties to the local power structure clearly make a difference. Village Creek is a case in point. With significant weak ties to surrounding areas, it could have more effectively responded to territorial threats in the aftermath of the Dursban release. The high density and homogeneity characteristic of the local ecology, however, promotes the absence of such ties, thereby reducing residents' ability to protect themselves against these kinds of risk.

Another aspect of local ecology, impacting support or protection, is the level of *territorial functioning* in the local area. If people feel strongly attached to a place (dwelling, block, or neighborhood) and trust their neighbors, they will more likely function territorially. This may be exhibited in behaviors ranging from increased maintenance of their surroundings to assisting their neighbors. Territorial functioning spills over into strong neighborhood ties. In communities where the neighborhood becomes a central behavioral space, community ties strengthen and the area becomes more capable of defending itself against outside threats. Certain ecological conditions promote or reduce territorial functioning. These include spatial conditions that make neighborhoods defensible, such as opportunities for residential surveillance; attractive exteriors; real barriers that separate the residential area into manageable sectors; the absence of "spatial incivilities" such as litter, dilapidation, and graffiti; and the presence of shrubs, trees, and gardens (Perkins, Brown, and Taylor 1996). In addition to these physical characteristics, a high concentration of transients in an area is likely to reduce trust, leading to lower identification with neighbors, and limited territorial functioning.

When these features of defensibility are absent, ties to the larger metropolitan area and local community may be affected. For example, spaces that fail to promote defensibility discourage local social interaction. Even under circumstances of high homogeneity and density, normal opportunities to develop a "communal" residential setting may be thwarted. Thus, local territorial functioning may be further discouraged, and potentially communal neighborhoods could experience detachment. According to Perkins and associates (1996) "spatial incivilities, plantings, and barriers that create manageable spatial territories" are factors that are important in shaping local patterns of interaction. These simple, yet manageable aspects of local ecology determine whether the spatial context promotes isolation, and whether the local area is actively engaged with the larger political context or inactive and ineffective.

Conclusion

Social science theories to this point have not adequately integrated place into an understanding of the social forces that impinge on the general health and well-being of individuals and populations. A review of the four major social theories of health provides a necessary backdrop for integrating basic ecological concepts into a more comprehensive approach to health and health behavior. This approach is particularly relevant to understanding the etiology and dynamics of the "urban health penalty." Certain neighborhoods within the United States clearly have distinct spatial qualities that shape residents' health risks, health beliefs, and behaviors, as well as the formal and informal networks of protection and support. Identifying these ecological characteristics is an essential first step to developing comprehensive programs that minimize or eliminate the urban health penalty. The value of this spatial approach derives not only from the ability to identify critical, yet often underexplored aspects of health, but also from the fact that spatial structures are more easily manipulated than social structures. Thus an ecology of health becomes both a useful and essential ingredient in a comprehensive health policy attending to the extraordinary needs of the inner city and its residents.

5

Cities as Mosaics of Risk and Protection

*For inner city children, the risks of living in the midst of vio-
lence are compounded by the risks of living in poverty—
risks that include malnutrition, unsuitable housing, infe-
rior medical care, inadequate schools, family disruption,
family violence, and maladaptive child-rearing patterns.*

DR. JAMES GARBARINO

*A silent war is being waged against Black and Latino
neighborhoods. Slowly we are being picked off by industries that don't give a damn about polluting our neighborhood, contaminating our water, fouling our air, clogging
our streets with big garbage trucks and lowering our property values.*

CHARLES STREADIT

a s noted in Chapter 3, inner-city neighborhoods
have undergone dramatic transformation in the
last several decades (Harris and Wilkins 1988;
Massey 1990; Massey and Denton 1987, 1993; Wilson 1987, 1996).
The concentration of poverty and the segregation of neighborhoods by

race and class have been powerful forces in the reshaping of metropolitan areas and their central cities. Poverty-stricken neighborhoods have become an all too common feature of the modern metropolis; by the early 1990s nearly 35 percent of urban residents were living in census tracts where at least 40 percent of residents had poverty-level incomes (Farley 1991; Massey and Denton 1993). These same neighborhoods tended to be racially stratified, with the average Black family, for example, living in census tracts where 30 percent of residents were poor. While the percentages vary for different racial and ethnic groups, there is a shared reality— nearly 90 percent of all residents in poor neighborhoods are members of a racial or ethnic minority (Jargowsky and Bane 1991).

With this high concentration of minority persons, underclass neighborhoods have become mainstays of the urban area. The so-called inner city is typically characterized as a place with relatively high average values on several poverty indicators: (1) working-age males without jobs, (2) households headed by women with children, (3) households receiving welfare, and (4) dropouts among the school-age population (Ricketts and Mincy 1990). The multidimensional character of poor neighborhoods implies potentially profound effects on the health and well-being of residents (Geronimus et al. 1997; LaViest 1993; LeClere, Rogers, and Peters 1997, 1998). With its youngest residents at greatest risk, inner-city communities have experienced a steady increase in the number of parents and young children living in poverty, an escalation in the number of female-headed households, expanding unemployment, and welfare dependency despite general national trends in the opposite direction, and a continual battle with rising crime and rampant drug abuse (Garbarino et al. 1992; Wilson 1987, 1996).

When the problems confronting urban residents are examined, some are structural factors, elements beyond the control of the individual, which have the capacity to affect large numbers of individuals and families. These structural effects are not evenly distributed, but rather are geographically concentrated such that where one lives—especially, where one grows up—exerts a profound effect on one's life chances, general health, and well-being (LeClere et al. 1997, 1998; Logan and Molotch 1987; Massey and Denton 1993; National Research Council 1993; Smith 1988).

The present chapter focuses specifically on the unevenly distributed hazards and risks confronting residents within metropolitan areas, as well as the layers of protection available to assist them in moderating the negative impact of these risks. As discussed in Chapter 1, hazards represent the circumstances and physical conditions that may produce harm in a population. On the other hand, risks represent the probability that certain individuals or groups will be harmed in their environment. Both hazard and risk are differentially distributed across residential areas in a metropolis, suggesting that levels of harm have a spatial component. The role that space plays in affecting exposure to hazards and risks is complicated by the fact that place is socially and culturally structured. Hence, the roles of salient social identities such as race, ethnicity, and class are confounded by hazards and risk inherent in certain places.

Uncertainty is characteristic of inner-city urban life. Understanding this uncertainty, its effects on health and well-being, and the availability of services and programs designed to protect persons from the consequences of this pervasive uncertainty is critical to addressing the health-place connection.

Physical Hazards and Risks in the Residential Environment

There is a growing recognition that disadvantaged populations are disproportionately exposed to a wide range of environmental health hazards threatening their general physical health and well-being (American Lung Association 1998; Bullard 1990, 1993; Edelstein 1988; Krieger et al. 1993; Rogers 1992; Williams 1996). Minority populations, particularly African American and Hispanic, are at risk for exposure to high levels of environmental contaminants not because of some inherent genetic characteristics or behavioral patterns, but rather because of the places where they live and work. More so than other racial or ethnic groups, they disproportionately live in areas that are noncompliant with national air-quality standards. For example, during the period between 1991 and 1993, an estimated 12.1 million children under the age of 13 were living in areas that did not meet current national ozone standards; almost 70 percent of those children were either African American or Hispanic (American Lung Association 1998).

The problem is not limited to the issue of air quality. When examining other forms of pollution (water, noise, toxic and hazardous waste), the statistical and practical realities are similar—socioeconomic conditions and race appear to be the major factors in determining exposure to multiple environmental hazards (Mohai and Bryant 1992; U.S. Environmental Protection Agency 1992; Williams 1996). Many of these environmental hazards are directly related to population growth and density, which are at their highest levels in the nation's urban areas: More than 75 percent of the U.S. population now lives in 283 census-designated metropolitan areas.

One such hazard is noise pollution. Estimates suggest that more than 12 million people are currently living in areas exceeding the federal maximum noise level standard of 55 decibels (U.S. Environmental Protection Agency 1991). Leading sources of this pollution include road, air, and train traffic, construction, manufacturing, and recreation. Regardless of the source, urban residents are more at risk for exposure to abnormally high levels of noise than their suburban or rural counterparts. This excessive risk, while not limited to poor and minority urban dwellers, is higher in urban neighborhoods with multifamily dwellings and apartments located closer to freeways, airports, and manufacturing. Thus by default, noise pollution becomes an unavoidable hazard for the special populations of the urban area such as minorities, poor, homeless, and other high-risk groups.

This hazard is important because of the health risks associated with chronic exposure to noise pollution. Although the major cause of noise-induced hearing loss is occupational, substantial damage has been noted through nonoccupational sources (NIOSH 1973). Besides hearing loss, a number of other conditions have been linked to excessive exposure to noise: sleep disturbance, hypertension, coronary disease, ulcers, colitis, depression, and anxiety (Kryter 1971). Few studies have examined the sociodemographic correlates of noise exposure and its effects on special populations. However, evidence does suggest that lower-income and minority residents, because they have fewer options of where to live, are at high risk of being exposed and adversely affected by this particular environmental hazard (U.S. Environmental Protection Agency 1977).

The health-related problems inherent in other forms of pollution are just as telling and perhaps even more problematic. Toxic waste dumping, water pollution, and runoff are other examples of hazards with significant physical and mental health consequences, particularly for the disadvantaged and underserved subpopulations living in inner cities. One study, *Toxic Wastes and Race in the United States* (Commission for Racial Justice, United Church of Christ 1987), describes the extent of discrimination and the consequences for those exposed to a wide range of pollutants. The study's conclusions are troubling: (1) Race is a significant factor associated with the location of hazardous waste; (2) the greatest number of commercial hazardous facilities are located in communities with the highest composition of racial and ethnic minorities; (3) three out of every five Hispanics or African Americans lived in communities with one or more toxic waste sites; and (4) low-income and minority populations were three times more likely to be drinking from a contaminated water supply than their upper-income White counterparts.

These conclusions underscore the importance of examining the connection between physical risk and the residential location of low-income and minority subpopulations. The tendency for low-income, minority communities to serve as sites for hazardous waste facilities suggests that the more economically depressed and desperate an area, the less capable it is of recognizing and rejecting such hazards (Gould 1998). Industry is likely to search out areas where resistance to placement of hazards is low. Communities with reduced access to economic opportunities are vulnerable to, and more accepting of, the health and environmental costs of hazard placement (Krieg 1998). In such areas, private industries manage to frame hazard placement as a benefit rather than a health risk, reducing the chances of consciousness-raising and local political mobilization. Besides these communities' economic disadvantages, however, places with concentrated minority poverty are disadvantaged by their network structures, which typically have limited ties to the outside (see Chapter 3). This absence of "weak ties" often prevents successful mobilization. Communities that can mobilize local institutions and grassroots support are more capable of offsetting private industries' ability to frame hazard dump location as a benefit, and more likely to prevent placement of the dump in their area (Gould 1998).

Indeed, significant changes can occur in communities when the relationship between place and health becomes highlighted and communities become involved in mobilizing against external threats. The first environmental discrimination lawsuit was filed in Houston in 1979, charging that Browning-Ferris Industries had targeted an African-

American neighborhood for the placement of a municipal solid-waste landfill. The argument was that this represented only one example of a long-term pattern of environmental racism in the city of Houston. Since the early 1920s, five Houston landfills and six of its eight incinerators had been placed in predominantly African-American neighborhoods. While the lawsuit failed, it represented a significant first step in the development of an environmental justice movement (Bullard 1990, 1993).

> The existence of a newly emergent environmental justice movement organized and controlled by communities of color, with support of local churches networked regionally and nationally and with a history of effective consciousness-raising and political conflict with more structurally powerful social actors may indeed have the capacity to repel private capital interests seeking to externalize hazards in minority communities. This may in fact be sending capital to look at less politically conscious and mobilized communities where local access to economic options may be slightly greater but potential resistance slightly lower. (Gould 1998:23)

The experiences of residents living along Village Creek have been very similar to the experiences of persons living in hundreds of other American urban communities. The health of these residents continues to be challenged by the environmental hazards produced by underregulated polluting industries. Evidence continues to accumulate establishing the role of environmental hazards in the physical and mental health of those at greatest risk (Brown and Mikkelsen 1990; Edelstein 1988; LaViest 1993; LeClere, Rogers, and Peters 1997, 1998; Rogers 1992). While recognition of the unequal distribution of risk is not new, the environmental justice movement has provided a framework for more effective advocacy. This framework allows local neighborhoods and action committees to organize and establish a voice, while at the same time forcing corporations to be more responsible for their actions and location decisions.

Sociocultural Hazards and Risks

A rich tradition of research, pioneered by the Chicago School of urban sociology (Park, Burgess, and McKenzie 1925), has established the existence of a relationship between community structure and various aspects of quality of life. From an early catalog of community characteristics (heterogeneity, segregation, density, and mobility) to a more intricate analysis of community social organization (social networks, organizational density, community cohesiveness, etc.), research supports the core hypothesis that social structural factors explain variations in rates of crime and delinquency within communities (Bursik and Grasmick 1993; Sampson and Lauritsen 1994; Reiss and Roth 1993; Shaw and McKay 1942).

The classic work of Shaw and McKay (1942) on the ecology of crime and delinquency led to the conclusion that the combination of three structural factors—low socioeconomic status, ethnic heterogeneity, and residential mobility—created residential environments characterized by community disorganization and high levels of crime and delinquency. Since then, researchers have continued to work on isolating the environmental characteristics which contribute to high levels of deviance and its consequences for the community and its residents (e.g., Beasely and Antunes 1974; Sampson and Lauritsen 1994). There is some disagreement over the existence of independent community subcultures and their role in propagating systems of norms and values that promote deviant behavior. Recent literature stresses the creative roles which individuals and groups can play in overcoming even the most negative environments (Wagner 1993). Nevertheless, researchers generally conclude that even though conventional norms dominate most communities, subcultural differences do exist with a tolerance of crime and deviant behavior clearly varying across structural and situational contexts (Sampson 1997).

Perhaps the best evidence to support the assumptions of a subcultural explanation originates from early research on juvenile delinquency, specifically juvenile gang violence (Cloward and Ohlin 1960; Cohen 1955, 1972; Miller 1958). This early work posited that gang behavior was, in part, a manifestation of the general cultural patterns of behavior embodied in the class structure. Certain areas of the city became breeding grounds for delinquency and gang behavior because of the underlying values of violence reinforced and maintained among adults and youth residing in those communities.

Recent ethnographic work (Anderson 1990; Jankowski 1991) supports this view and illustrates how the persistence of poverty reinforces acceptance of the necessity and the role of community violence among neighborhood residents. Both authors, while examining different Chicago ethnic communities, suggest that socially disorganized poor communities developed a culture that legitimized and glorified deviance and crime. Thus in some contexts, the dominant cultural norms and values became irrelevant, superceding a new set of rules prescribing behavior. This new set of rules, the "code of the streets," regulates violent behavior, and establishes rules and regulations for code enforcement. Though often opposed by families and friends, a child's familiarity with the code tends to be more subtly encouraged in order to help them negotiate the risky circumstances of the inner-city environment (Anderson 1997).

In addition to the cultural determinants of risky behavior, researchers have identified physical characteristics that are key markers for hazardous, high-risk environments (Lynn and McGeary 1990; Reiss and Roth 1993; Sampson and Lauritsen 1994; Taylor and Covington 1988; Taylor and Gottfredson 1986). Studies suggest that these places can include public spaces near apartments or other multifamily dwellings, vacant lots and buildings, areas with high rates of geographic mobility and family instability, and street designs that allow for "open-air" drug markets to develop. These markets have the physical characteristics of narrow one-way streets with physical cover, easy and multiple escape routes, vacant building and lots, and landscape shapes that enable smooth-flowing drug traffic as well as a careful surveillance of police activity (Reiss and Roth 1993). Public areas near multifamily dwellings are notoriously difficult areas to monitor, posing significant threats to adults and young children alike. Keeping safe in such high-hazard areas is a task not unlike that of the soldier trying to survive on the open battlefield.

Alex Kotlowitz (1991), in his story *There Are No Children Here,* writes about the "killing fields" in and around a large multifamily unit in Chicago, the backdrop for his tale of two brothers and their struggle to survive inner-city life.

> On the city's near west side, on the periphery of one of the city's black ghettoes, was built Henry Horner Homes. The buildings were constructed on the cheap. There were no lobbies to speak of, only the open breezeways. There was no

communication system from the breezeways to the tenants. During the city's harsh winters, elevator cables froze; in one year alone the housing authority in Chicago needed to make over fifteen hundred elevator repairs. And that was just in one development.

The trash chutes within each building were too narrow to handle the garbage from all of its tenants. The boiler system continually broke down. There were insufficient lighting installations and wall outlets in each unit. (p. 22)

Not only are the buildings a problem for the residents, but so, too, are the general design and use of the housing project:

Henry Horner's buildings range from seven to fifteen stories and cover eight blocks. The architect surely had an easy time designing the development, for it is only one block wide, leaving little room for experimentation with the placement of high-rises. The buildings, with few exceptions, line each side of the block, leaving the corridor in between for playground equipment, basketball courts, and parking lots. A narrow street once cut through the development's midsection, but that has long since been displaced and is now part of the concrete play area. At first, that pleased the parents, who worried about their children getting hit by speeding cars, but later it served to isolate parts of the complex even more, making it easier for criminals to operate with impunity. (p. 25)

Clearly, the lack of defensible space is a critical issue for many housing projects in urban areas throughout the United States. Several prescriptions have been offered for reducing the risk of crime and violence by altering the physical environment (Newman 1973a, 1975), but in practice their effects are modest.

While alterations in the physical environment make some difference, perhaps a more critical factor in assessing risk exposure is behavioral—people taking unnecessary risks and engaging in health-compromising behavior. For example, "lifestyle" and "routine activities" theories both propose that an individual's activities affect their level of risk. Thus, the more likely people are to come into contact with potential perpetrators in physical spaces where no one can intervene, the greater the likelihood of victimization (Cohen and Felson 1979; Hindelang, Gottfredson, and Garofalo 1978). Empirical evidence in support of this general hypothesis is indirect; nevertheless, there appears to be a statistical relationship between specific behaviors/personal characteristics and violent victimization. Teenagers or young adults who are unemployed, from low-income households, and spend considerable time outdoors during the evening hours, particularly in high-risk physical settings (parks, abandoned buildings, vacant lots, etc.), are at greater risk of becoming victims of violence.

While persons modify their behaviors when confronted with extreme danger, those modifications are often not sufficient to offset the general environmental risks present in certain communities and neighborhoods (Miethe and Meier 1990). The fact is, most criminal acts require a convergence of behavioral, physical, and social factors. Obviously, some environments are more conducive to crime than others; the presence of certain factors will either promote or constrain criminal behaviors (Miethe and McDowall 1993). A fundamental assumption underlying the contextual approach to risk-taking behavior is that risk is at least partially a function of social forces operating outside the individual and closely tied to various aspects of space.

Blankets of Protection

Though the physical and psychological risks associated with certain urban spaces and places are substantial, layers of formal and informal protection attached to place help to insulate residents from myriad environmental challenges. These layers of protection moderate the negative effects of environmental stressors and risks on a variety of health-related outcomes. On the basis of this relationship, we can pose several questions concerning the role of protection in understanding the place-health relationship. Are levels of protection similar for all residents, or do they vary by sociodemographic characteristics? Do they vary by place? Are formal and informal sources of protection more important for some populations living in some places compared to others? What role does the health care system play in moderating risk's impact on particular populations living in certain places?

Over the years, a considerable body of research has developed point-ing to the critical role of the family in the overall development of chil-dren (e.g., Bandura 1986; Baumrind and Black 1967; Bronfenbrenner 1986; Escalona 1982; Rutter 1987). Family and the home can provide models for learning, as well as protective environments during develop-ment. However, they may also create significant problems for the child in both early and later life. In fact, research shows that one of the best predictors of health-compromising behavior among young persons is an unstable family structure with moderately high levels of family discord (Heatherington and Camara 1984; National Research Council 1993; Reiss and Roth 1993). Children from single-parent families are two to three times more likely than children of two-parent families to have emotional difficulties (Dornbusch and Gray 1988; Fitzpatrick and Boldizar 1993; McLanahan 1986; National Research Council 1993). In addition, children from unstable family units are more likely to drop out of high school, become pregnant as teenagers, abuse drugs, and have criminal records either as a juvenile or adult (National Center for Health Statistics 1990).

With health risks high in inner-city environments, the role of the fam-ily as a protector becomes even more crucial. While family structure is clearly important, other characteristics and dynamics of the family are equally important in moderating health outcomes. "Family protection" comprises a nurturing family environment, parental promotion of learn-ing, a multigenerational kin network, dependable child care in the absence of parents, warm, close relationships with parents, absence of marital and family conflict, significant attention and stimulation during the first year of life, and clear behavioral guidelines and expectations. Hawkins and his colleagues define the importance of family as a protec-tive factor in preventing or moderating health-compromising, risk-taking behaviors such as drug and alcohol abuse (Hawkins 1995; Hawkins, Catalano, and Miller 1992; Hawkins and Weis 1985). Their work indicates that even in the face of overwhelming odds, some chil-dren exhibit a remarkable degree of resilience when they have the pro-tection of family, friends, and the larger community. These environmental safeguards enhance youths' ability to resist stressful life events and help promote social adaptation and competence necessary for survival and success (Garmezy 1983; Jessor 1993; Werner 1990).

Thus, at least one parent or reference person, a strong social network outside the family, a supportive educational climate, and a community that provides opportunities and resources for parents and children are necessary assets creating an "environment of support" conducive to adaptation.

Unfortunately, many of these protective factors are not typically present in families, particularly those families facing the challenges of raising children in poverty, with a single parent (usually a mother who works outside the home), displaced networks of support, and inadequate formal support services. In these cases, the mental and physical health risks of children are elevated and the life of the community as a whole becomes threatened. As the architect of the "War on Poverty," President Lyndon Johnson reminded us:

> The family is the cornerstone of our society. More than any other force it shapes the attitude, the hopes, the ambitions, and the values of the child. And when the family is threatened or collapses, it is the children that are usually damaged. When it happens on a massive scale the community itself is crippled. (commencement address, Howard University, 1965)

Beyond the risk and protective factors literature, a substantial literature in the sociology of mental health convincingly argues for the role of social support in moderating the negative effects of stressors on individual's mental and physical health (Cohen 1988; Ensel and Lin 1991; Lin et al. 1986; Thoits 1984, 1995; Vaux 1988). Informal networks of support including family, friends, relatives, co-workers, and neighbors provide instrumental, informational, and emotional assistance that can combat the negative effects of stress. The character and overall impact of this support as a stress moderator varies by place of residence as well as the person's attachment to that community.

Extensive research on social support leads to three major conclusions regarding its role in promoting health and well-being. First, support is directly and positively related to health, but it does not buffer the negative impact of stressful life events or chronic strains on health. Thus, while support clearly influences health, its role as a stress buffer is debatable (e.g., Ensel and Lin 1991). A substantial body of research suggests that support mediates, rather than buffers, the negative effect of stress on health outcomes. The distinction appears minor. It is an important one, however, with very different implications for health outcomes (Ensel and Lin 1991; Thoits 1995; Wheaton 1985). Second, perceived support, even more than actual support, is directly related to better physical and mental health. A perception of strong support from others moderates the negative effects of life events and chronic strains on one's physical and mental health. Third, the most powerful aspect of support appears to be whether or not a person has an intimate, confiding relationship with another person (spouse, lover, friend, etc.). Having a confidant is extremely important for stress reduction, particularly among persons such as the urban elderly, spatially segregated minorities, and others who may not have an extensive social network.

General social support research is informative, providing a good deal of insight into the psychosocial dynamics of health outcomes. However, it doesn't provide much information about the role of place in the provision of social support or its subsequent impact on health. A spatial analysis focusing on the neighborhood and the neighbor's role seems particularly relevant for articulating an "ecology of health" approach.

The Neighborhood

Throughout history the neighborhood has functioned as a place for exchange and mutual aid, meeting both the psychological and material needs of residents (LaGory and Pipkin 1981). At the same time, industrialization and subsequent community development profoundly changed the ways in which individuals communicate and associate with one another, and as a result, neighboring itself was transformed (Keller 1968). The neighborhood was no longer as spatially bounded as activities, work, and the rules of social exchange changed. What happened? Why did the neighborhood change, and what was responsible for that change?

1. As mobility increased, due to mass transportation improvements, the activity space of community members multiplied, permitting social networks to spatially expand beyond the neighborhood boundary.

2. Mass media and communication networks improved, making sources of information more accessible; reliance on neighbors for information declined.

3. An increasing division of labor led to diversification in interests and work cycles, lowering both residents' availability and desire to interact with neighbors.

4. A growth in formally organized social services and an increase in economic security lowered the need for neighbors to rely on one another for assistance, particularly in times of economic crisis.

5. The shift from extended to nuclear families produced a family unit whose needs were less localized and could often be met by other institutions.

Over time, the rules of neighboring shifted. The often "taken for granted" expectation of neighbors watching over one another, moving freely from one front porch to another, and sometimes relying on informal neighbor networks for information and assistance was no longer present. The neighborhood appeared to be dissolving, as Tönnies ([1887] 1957) and Wirth (1938) had predicted. Their *urbanism* tradition argued that the changes produced by industrialization caused close community ties to be substituted with secondary ones. More contemporary research seems to support this general notion (Campbell and Lee 1992; Wellman, 1979), and while close interaction among neighbors is not a lost art, it has been supplemented for many by intimacy that stretches beyond the physical boundary of the neighborhood (Granovetter 1973a and b; LaGory and Pipkin 1981).

In addition to neighborhood dynamics, we also should recognize that the content of informal support, and how it gets delivered, is not constant across all communities but determined in part by the characteristics of place. Thus, some inner-city neighborhoods create an "atmosphere of learning" unlike that found in other areas of the metropolis. Typically, individuals are exposed to a range of recurring ghetto-related behaviors that, while viewed as adaptive, may have negative consequences. Displays of violence, public drinking, and idleness are present in many underclass inner-city neighborhoods, and while denounced by many, the behaviors are allowed to occur. Their occurrence is a function of the larger social organization's failure to control the behaviors, and of a cultural milieu that enables it (Wilson 1996). Purposeful or accidental, cultural transmission creates a set of values and beliefs that are damaging to the future of any place.

On the other hand, Mitchell Duneier (1992), in his book *Slim's Table,* attempts to illustrate the other, more beneficial side to cultural transmission when he examines role modeling as a lost form of support in the restructuring of the Black community. In weaving a story about companionship, sharing, and caring among a group of Black and White men meeting at a Chicago South Side cafeteria, Valois, Duneier shows how this inner-city working class group embodies a set of traditional values that translates into a way of life and responsibility. These men acknowledge their role in teaching, supporting, encouraging, and caring for those around them, particularly young inner-city men who must acknowledge their responsibility to work, their families, and their larger community.

Formal Support Services

The city can be characterized "as a gigantic man-made resource system which contains an abundance of resources for individuals and families to exploit for their own benefit" (Harvey 1972:3). While the city is a resource machine, it is important to remember that access to this machine is spatially constrained. Resources are not equally distributed across the urban landscape; critical resources are more accessible to some than to others. Segregation's impact on the delivery of services is an important illustration of the role of places in determining access to goods and services, and in turn, influencing health outcomes.

The costs incurred by the "urban health penalty" are significant. The most dramatic illustration of its costs can be seen in how health care services are distributed across the metropolitan area. Inner cities are characterized as islands of illness and premature death. These places suffer the brunt of the AIDS epidemic, outbreaks of tuberculosis and hepatitis A, sexually transmitted diseases, measles, and general cancers (Aday 1993; Geiger 1992). Death comes sooner, more frequently, and often because of inadequate treatment.

Beyond the risks related to specific health conditions in core urban communities, weakening urban social and economic structures further contribute to the health penalty, and place the poor, minorities, homeless, and other core residents at greater risk. Relying on the hospital

emergency room as their primary care provider, many residents
encounter major problems with health care, and access is threatened
when local urban hospitals have difficulty competing with suburban
complexes and sometimes must close their doors. Since the late 1970s
and early 1980s, large urban areas have lost many of their local hospitals
(Sager 1983; Whiteis 1992, 1997). The irony of this trend points to a
major problem facing the inner cities. On the one hand, these communities are the very places where preventive and primary care is needed most.
Patients here tend to be sicker and are often without health insurance.
Yet, on the other hand, hospitals and health care facilities are overbur-
dened in these communities and have a much lower profit margin than
those located in the suburbs. Thus access becomes a critical issue for
many, and the withdrawal of services is another instance of the penalty
that low-income minority residents pay for their residential location.

To further illustrate this serious tear in the "blanket of protection," a
recent study of nine low-income minority communities in New York
City, one off which was Harlem, found:

> The main victims in Harlem are working age adults.
> Compared to the rest of New York City, the death rate for
> people aged 15–44 in Harlem was 240 percent higher; for
> those 44–65, it was 128 percent higher. These were not
> deaths that arose from violence and drugs; the leading killers
> in Harlem were cancer, heart attack, hypertensive disease,
> pneumonia, diabetes, bronchitis. Not coincidentally, this is
> the same community that is documented here to have four
> fully functioning physicians to provide basic health care for
> its 214,000 inhabitants. (Brelloche and Carter 1990:iv)

Government-sponsored support is available in communities like
Harlem, yet the support never seems to be in direct proportion to the
need. Indicative of "territorial injustice," the penalty of residence in certain parts of the urban area is notably severe, and official sources of protection often lax.

Nevertheless, protection and support is available from a variety of
nonprofits, schools, churches, as well as community and neighborhood
initiatives. This safety net further defines the nature of available "formal
support" in the urban area. One excellent example of a nonprofit mak-

ing the difference in the fight against the "urban penalty" is Habitat for Humanity. This organization, founded by Millard Fuller in the early 1980s, has as part of its mission a proposal "to eliminate poverty and substandard housing in the United States" (Fuller 1995). Perhaps better than any other organization, operating in all 50 states and worldwide in nearly 50 countries, Habitat understands the connection between place and health. Whether it is a community with a weakened infrastructure or a blighted neighborhood with no decent housing, Habitat stresses the importance of place in countering the impact of poverty on health and well-being. Fuller not only sees the critical links between concentrated poverty and health, but fervently believes that unhealthy places can be transformed. They can be transformed physically, socially, and spiritually into areas where people can thrive. Providing decent, affordable housing, he argues, can be a prescription for a healthier society.

Living in substandard housing can be a sickening experience—literally. In a recently published report by Children's Hospital in Boston, *Not Safe at Home,* researchers focused on poor housing as a children's health issue, identifying specific aspects of housing which present threats to the health and well-being of residents (Sandel and Sharfstein 1998). Citing health problems ranging from lead poisoning to asthma and other respiratory diseases, the report spells out the importance of working toward alternative housing solutions. Habitat, more so than any other nonprofit organization, has responded to this need and continues to build affordable, decent housing around the world. By 1997, Habitat had contributed to a "blanket of protection," building nearly 50,000 homes in the United States that shelter more than a quarter of a million people. It is a powerful example of how a single organization can make a difference in creating and revitalizing places within the inner city. In the process, it has become an effective tool for health promotion in inner-city and aging suburban neighborhoods.

Thousands of other nonprofit groups continue to carve out niches in the local support system, meeting the needs of special populations. Homeless shelters for men, women, and children have increased significantly over the last two decades. In a comprehensive study of homelessness during the 1980s, Burt (1992a and b) gathered data that showed an impressive growth in the number of shelters and shelter beds during the period between 1981 and 1989. In cities wth populations of more than

100,000 in every region of the country, both the numbers and rates of homelessness, shelters, and shelter beds increased nearly threefold over this period of time. By the end of the decade, there were nearly 1,500 shelters serving almost 200,000 persons (Burt 1992a and b). The piecemeal programs offered there, however, cannot begin to meet the complex needs of the urban dispossessed.

United Way agencies supporting the homeless and hundreds of other causes continue to struggle to meet the needs of those challenged by residing in declining urban environments. Nonprofit agencies find their budgets stretched to the limit each year as urban crises expand and new problems develop. In an effort to help fill the gap, churches have responded by developing comprehensive programs addressing a myriad of problems endemic to inner-city populations. With more than 330,000 churches and synagogues and a membership of more than 150 million people, these organizations represent a powerful network of social-service delivery (Claman, Butler, and Boyatt 1994). Nonprofit and government agencies are largely responsible for the bulk of service delivery to those in greatest need. Their resources, however, are limited, and the needs of some populations often go beyond what is available. Outreach is a natural extension of the church and the development of a faith community. Thus, churches have provided a vision of assistance that sometimes supersedes even the most visionary nonprofit agency or government leader.

Traditionally, churches have provided care and assistance to the elderly; food, clothing and shelter to the homeless and poor; health care to the elderly and poor; educational programs for youths; jobs and income assistance to the poor; housing and housing rehabilitation to neighborhoods; and infrastructural assistance to communities in need around the world. Exemplary programs abound in the community of faith. One example of a successful, long-standing program is the Central Health Center in Atlanta, Georgia. Started in 1922 by the Central Presbyterian Church, the health clinic now serves more than 6,000 patients a year. It provides basic treatment, physical exams, family planning, dental care, counseling, and a pharmacy. Another example can be found in Birmingham, Alabama, where the Cooperative Downtown Ministries, a collection of inner-city churches, has provided dental services, shelter, physician access, transportation, job training, and access to comprehensive drug and alcohol treatment programs for thousands of homeless since the early 1980s. Hundreds of other examples around the country illustrate the important "safety net role" that churches can play in meeting the needs of special populations who fall through the formal service-delivery net. Recent research suggests that in addition to providing basic services, churches can play an effective role in motivating the larger community to participate in place-based interventions (Davis et al. 1994).

In addition to the church, government intervention has addressed problems plaguing the inner city. Government-sponsored housing, community development programs, Job Corps, Healthy Start, Head Start, and VISTA all have played a role in problem management and assistance for special populations. Government, however, also has been responsible for the production of concentrated poverty and the divided city.

Dating back to the Great Depression and the New Deal, governments shaped the direction and evolution of urban space. Generally, the purpose was twofold: 1) to encourage home ownership and 2) to improve living conditions for low-income groups (through, for example, rent control, public housing, and urban renewal). The first goal was largely successful as middle- to upper-class residents found refuge in newly developed suburban areas on the fringe of the city. Unfortunately, homeowners moved from a declining central-city housing market and infrastructure, leaving the lower class behind and promoting income segregation across the metropolitan area. In effect, successful home-ownership programs for the middle class eventually made living conditions for some segments of the poor worse rather than better. For example, though urban renewal was designed to greatly improve the quality of low-income neighborhoods, it eventually promoted an urban spatial structure that gave way to social injustice and segregation (LaGory and Pipkin 1981). Thus while some effort was made to attract the middle class back to the central city and reconstruct the tax base, large areas of dilapidated housing were cleared and thousands of residents displaced (Porteous 1977). By attacking the physical expressions of poverty in the city and not the underlying issues themselves, urban renewal became a tool of the federal government for maintaining the status quo of poverty in the city.

One important agent of protection that has been very successful in aiding and supporting the population of the inner city has been the school. While inner-city schools continue to struggle with low achievement scores, high dropout rates, high personnel turnover, administrative overhead, declining facilities, and a shrinking tax base, they remain one of the most durable and available forms of local protection. Schools traditionally have sought to protect youths, yet in recent years many school systems have expanded their "programs of protection" to include young adult education and, more recently, the "command center" for communitywide prevention and intervention programs. One example of the change that has taken place in the last few decades is the establishment of hospital satellite clinics and hospital-based adolescent clinics that make health care more accessible to youths (Walter et al. 1995).

The growth of the school-based health clinic has been a natural extension of this recent outreach trend; currently there are more than 1,100 clinics serving students in 41 states (McKinney and Peak 1994; Schlitt 1994). With a specific design for reaching underserved youths, school clinics serve as an important medical catchall in inner-city areas that are often unable to furnish comprehensive medical services to this difficult-to-reach population. The school clinic provides acute care for minor illnesses, reproductive care, screening for and treatment of chronic illnesses, mental health counseling, immunizations, and health promotion. While parents and community leaders continue to be concerned about the clinic as a distribution point for birth control devices and the implicit promotion of adolescent sexuality, these clinics have proved to be a critical point in the delivery of medical services to youth. These important models of school health manage to incorporate all aspects of health promotion with a focus on multilevel, comprehensive educational programs (Hacker et al. 1994).

Beyond medical care, schools also attempt to help low-achieving students by providing specific programs to address student motivation, dropout prevention, grade failure, drug and alcohol use, and violence. Chapter 1 programs (previously Title 1) have existed since 1965, when the federal government made a substantial financial and organizational commitment to combat the problem of school dropouts. Nationally, the program serves more than 14,000 schools with a funding level in excess of $6 billion (Jennings 1991). Its primary focus is on low-income students. The evaluations of Chapter 1, however, have been mixed; while those schools and students touched by Chapter 1 programs have clearly improved, improvements appear modest compared to students enrolled in regular curricula (Kennedy, Jung, and Orland 1986). As a natural extension of Chapter 1, dropout prevention programs sprang up all over the country. By the end of the 1980s, there were nearly 1,000 dropout prevention programs operating in thousands of schools around the country. The majority of these were designed to target high-risk students for special services aimed at improving their academic performance, attitudes, and rates of absenteeism and tardiness (U.S. General Accounting Office 1987).

The strategy of preventing dropouts is important, particularly for urban schools. An estimated one-fourth of all urban schools have dropout rates of 50 percent or more, making individualized service, high school programs, and need-targeting no longer feasible (National Research Council 1993). The new focus of dropout prevention programs is to target students in early years (elementary and early middle school), reduce their alienation from the education process, and find ways to promote their interest in learning (Wehlage et al. 1989). Until schools address the problems of negative student perceptions and attempt to reduce the sense of student alienation in inner-city schools, it seems unlikely that these dropout prevention programs will be effective at motivating students to learn and to stay in school.

While schools represent an important component of protection, comprehensive community-based prevention and intervention programs exemplify cutting-edge service provision. Although a more detailed examination of these place-based delivery systems will be presented in Chapter 8, it is important to recognize their significance in providing protection in high-risk, inner-city settings. One example is the Safe Block Project in Philadelphia, Pennsylvania (Schwarz et al. 1993). The program designed a comprehensive injury-prevention trial focusing on home health hazards and injury knowledge in several poor, urban African-American neighborhoods. This injury-prevention effort was one of the first to successfully provide comprehensive prevention programs in extremely poor inner-city neighborhoods. With growing public outcries demanding community-level strategies for transforming the health risks in minority populations (Braithwaite et al. 1989; Hammond and Yung 1991), new place-based efforts must be developed.

Success stories abound for risk reduction programs addressing a variety of other problems. General prevention and demonstration studies show, for example, that the most promising approach to preventing alcohol and drug problems lies in coordinated prevention efforts that offer multiple strategies and multiple points of program access that promote participation by the full community (Office of Substance Abuse Prevention 1991). One of the underlying philosophical assumptions of the OSAP is that "the community is the best vehicle through which to develop and implement comprehensive prevention efforts." While this philosophy is important, its execution remains hampered by social, political, economic, psychological, and cultural barriers present in many low-income, minority, underserved communities across the country. The strategies that should be introduced to overcome these barriers, and to effectively address populations at risk and in need, is of critical import to the overall framework of this book and is addressed in Chapter 8.

Physical and Mental Health Consequences for the Urban Dweller

As seen in Chapters 3 and 4, health is intimately tied to place and the circumstances and conditions of place. Places are composed of unique combinations of risks and protection that, depending on their interaction with one another, create significant health consequences. Some populations may be more at risk than others; Chapters 6 and 7 detail some of those high-risk populations. The remainder of this chapter presents a brief overview of health consequences for the general urban dweller.

A recent report, released by the U.S. Department of Health and Human Services, indicates some progress in the improvement of national health statistics. Unfortunately, this progress has not been experienced uniformly (U.S. Health and Human Services 1998). Low-income persons, minorities, and urban residents had more health risk factors, including sedentary lifestyles, cigarette smoking, less health insurance coverage, and less preventive care. Thus, while some parts of the population have experienced improving health, the penalty for those unable to afford quality health care, or for those living in areas where access to health care services is restricted, continues to grow. This "urban health penalty" highlights the importance of addressing the multidimensional health problems endemic to inner-city populations.

While many factors contribute to the health status of inner-city residents, poverty is primary among them. Lack of good nutrition, homelessness, exposure to violence, substance abuse, inadequate housing, and limited access to health care are all indicators of an area under stress. For many, poverty increases the risk of contracting disease and facing an early death. Recent national statistics indicate that inner-city poverty had a much greater influence on cancer rates than either race or culture (Oakie 1991). Likewise, research reports significant cardiovascular mortality differences between women living in specific types of communities (low-income, predominantly minority, etc.), compared to the general population (LeClere et al. 1998).

Unfortunately, adverse physical health conditions have become a fact of life for many urban residents. Exposure to environmental hazards such as lead, toxic waste, and a variety of pollutants is extremely high in urban centers. Children between one and five years of age living in low-income, inner-city families are more than seven times as likely to have elevated lead levels in their blood as are children in other, less-threatening environments (U.S. Health and Human Services 1998). Poor, non-Hispanic Black children are at greatest risk, with more than 20 percent having high lead levels in their blood, compared to 8 percent for low-income White children. Inadequate housing is a significant contributor to lead poisoning, and according to a recent study, lead levels are highest among children living in housing more than 50 years old (Centers for Disease Control 1998). These pre–WW II buildings and houses are common in many older central cities in the Northeast and Midwest.

While the structural circumstances of inner-city areas produce risks for some residents, residents' social and behavioral characteristics also contribute to the negative health consequences of places. HIV is becoming more common in the inner city. In 1990, HIV was the leading cause of death for men ages 25 to 44 in 64 of 170 cities with more than 25 HIV deaths (Andrulis 1997). Alcohol and drug use continues to be a major health problem in the United States, with urban areas being particularly hard hit by an increasing concentration of addiction. In 1991, more than 25 million people reported using illegal drugs; much of that drug abuse was confined to inner-city neighborhoods (Musto 1987).

Another significant health risk for city residents is exposure to violence. City dwellers are twice as likely to be victims of violence, and murder rates are more than three times greater in central cities than other parts of the metropolitan area (Fingerhut and Kleinman 1990;

Reiss and Roth 1993; U.S. Health and Human Services 1998). Gang activity, drug traffic, weapon availability, unemployment, poverty, and a host of other social circumstances contribute to a violence epidemic which is clearly in need of control. It is essential to understand the role communities play in violence exposure. Communities can either insulate residents from the harmful effects of violence or exacerbate the risk of residents' exposure to violence (Levine and Rosich 1996). As discussed earlier, the physical and sociocultural characteristics of some places can be important predictors of health. Thus, regardless of their general sociodemographic makeup, structural attributes of communities can be important predictors of health-compromising behavior.

Youths are more susceptible to the adverse effects of urban violence exposure. Homicide rates among children have increased nearly 300 percent in the last 40 years; these increases are particularly pronounced among inner-city residents, especially males and African-Americans (National Research Council 1993; Prothrow-Stith 1991; Reiss and Roth 1993; Rosenberg and Fenley 1991). This increase is clearly a consequence of living in risky environments, some of which have become loci of criminal activities. Whether children are perpetrators or victims of violence, it is important to recognize that environmental circumstances can affect their developmental trajectories. A more detailed discussion of youth as ecological actors, and the role that context plays in their development, follows in Chapter 7.

Since the pioneering work of Chicago School sociologists (e.g., Faris and Dunham 1939), research has focused on the critical relationship between mental health problems and socioeconomic status (Dohrenwend and Dohrenwend 1969; Dohrenwend et al. 1992; Eaton 1986; Kessler and Neighbors 1986; Turner, Wheaton, and Lloyd 1995). This early research made us aware of the importance of the urban context in determining the mental and physical health status of residents. By examining the areal distribution of functional psychoses such as schizophrenia, they discovered a relationship between urban residential location and rates of mental illness (Faris and Dunham 1939). The highest rates of illness occurred near the central business district, with rates declining as distance from the urban core increased. This led researchers to conclude that there was in fact a pattern of illness directly related to place. Place and mental health were inextricably linked. As expected, areas with a high prevalence of disease were urban slums where concentrations of poverty, poor housing, crime, and homelessness were the greatest.

Some years later, Srole and associates (1962) conducted a mental-disorder-prevalence study in midtown Manhattan. They found significant differences in patterns of disorder distributed across varying socioeconomic groups living in different areas of the city. More recent research, while not as ambitious as these larger epidemiological surveys, is beginning to identify core relationships between mental health and social structure. Variation in individual exposure to stress has been documented by marital status, gender, race, and socioeconomic status (e.g., Turner et al. 1995). Social variation in mental health is, in part, a function of systematic differences in the quantity and nature of stress that individuals experience by being located in a variety of social situations and positions. Thus, stress is not just an individual risk factor; stress is seen as a link in a causal chain that starts with social conditions and ends with differences in risk for mental health problems (Aneshensel 1992). As Aneshensel argues, "Stress can be systemic—it may be tied to specific locations or social group experiences and not distributed randomly but rather predetermined by location or social position." Thus, just as the Chicago School anticipated, mental illness is distributed differentially across the urban landscape.

In fact, varying patterns of illness related to community/neighborhood contexts have been documented recently, opening the door for a more careful and thorough spatial analysis of illness and disease (Aneshensel 1992; Aneshensel and Sucoff 1996; Brooks-Gunn et al. 1993; Cockerham 1996; Crane 1991; Kessler et al. 1994). Researchers have started cataloging aspects of life in the urban area, attempting to find out how they contribute to mental health problems. As discussed in Chapter 2, overcrowding is one aspect of the urban environment identified as contributing to mental illness among urban dwellers, but studies of overcrowding have generated mixed results. Some research found modest relationships between neighborhood density and various aspects of mental illness. A number of studies concluded that overcrowding had its greatest impact within the home (Galle and Gove 1978; Gove et al. 1979), exacerbating negative circumstances already present there and contributing to a higher prevalence of mental disorders in areas with high household density (Cockerham 1996).

Conclusion

Inner cities are facing significant health challenges promoted by the dramatic divide characteristic of the late-twentieth-century urban landscape. Health status and access to services for low-income minority urban populations are significantly lower than those for the rest of the country. In some cases, the health of inner cities most closely resembles that of developing countries and shows little sign of improvement. The negative health image of the city is difficult to overcome. Addressing it requires the concerted efforts of local, regional, and national governments, private agencies, and health care organizations, which pool their resources to change the current status of "health in the city."

This chapter has attempted to provide an overview of the risks and protections that are products of places. Focusing on the unhealthy aspects of the inner city, a review of physical and sociocultural risks highlights the potential impact of these environmental irritants on physical and mental health. While risk and protection vary across the urban landscape, concentrations of risk are differentiated by class, race, age, and other sociodemographic characteristics of populations. Protection is characterized as a network of resources, both formal and informal, operating at a variety of levels to insulate individuals from the negative features of unhealthy places. Clearly, risk and protection affect residents' health in a variety of ways. The next two chapters examine risk and protection in more detail, focusing on the city's most vulnerable subpopulations—the homeless, racial minorities, youths, and the elderly.

6

Special Populations in the City

Needs and Risks of the Socially Disadvantaged

We have been—and remain—two nations: one majority, one minority—separated by the quality of our health.

DONNA SHALALA

Conservatives argue that the United States "won" the Cold War. . . . But the economy that won this victory cannot house its own people and condemns a significant percentage of them to a life of poverty and struggle. If this is victory, it is a hollow victory indeed.

JOEL BLAU

s larger and larger portions of American society access the Internet, the world appears to be at our fingertips. In this emerging "information society," where communication technologies expand the capacity for exchange almost exponentially, we seem to be approximating a situation in which, as a recent media campaign suggested, there will soon be "no there, there." But this world of immediate accessibility is illusory.

Indeed, as the information highway continues to give us the capacity for a truly global village, a new version of the divided society is emerging, with inequalities as dramatic and debilitating as any that have ever existed in human history.

We have demonstrated throughout this book that place continues to matter for everyone. As shown in this chapter and the next, however, place-based differences may actually be at the heart of a growing social divide. Despite the emergence of the spaceless realm in the information-based society, some groups remain very spatially dependent. In the next two chapters, we explore the special problems and needs of four groups, showing how spatial contexts interact with limited personal and social resources to constrain the opportunities and experiences of each group. In Chapter 6, we address the spatial challenges faced by two specific segments of the very poor—homeless populations, and urban racial/ethnic poor (African Americans). In Chapter 7, we show the unique person-environment challenges faced at the beginning and end of the life cycle, exploring the distinct spatial limitations of the very young and the very old.

Inequality and Health

This chapter deals with the significance of space and place for the health of the socially disadvantaged. Overwhelming evidence suggests that the already health-compromising circumstances of personal poverty are further exacerbated by the fact that the very poor often find themselves unavoidably "in the wrong place at the wrong time." Such is the story of the impoverished, predominantly African-American residents of Village Creek. It is also the picture presented in research on homeless persons where the stressful circumstances of placelessness are clearly demonstrated (LaGory, Richey, and Mullis 1990; Rossi 1989; Wright 1989).

Poverty and inequality, at an individual level, may be understood as stressors (Lin et al. 1986; Fox et al. 1985; Wilkinson 1996) that adversely affect the health of their victims. Such circumstances do lasting psychological and emotional damage to individuals and affect the home environment which, under more normal conditions, protects people from hazardous circumstances. Wilkinson (1996) argues that the most crucial factors in this relationship between poverty and health are not health care deficits but deteriorating social support systems, particularly within the domestic environment. Poverty erodes family support by creating stressors in the home that lead to dissension among family members, often translating into significant family problems and unhappy childhoods that have long-term repercussions for health and health behaviors (Lundberg 1993; Piliavin, Sosin, and Westerfelt 1993). The critical linkage between poverty, stress, and health may be less a function of income and more a result of the broader life circumstance that poverty represents. Place may be a better proxy than income for the overall decrement of well-being associated with poverty (Wilkinson 1996). In American society, place is a basic social identifier; it is the single most important product that we ever purchase. For the very poor, in some parts of the United States, housing comprises nearly 75 percent of total monthly expenditures.

Poverty's effect on health is not merely an individual-level phenomenon. As we have seen in Chapters 3 and 5, poverty is a place-based phenomenon. Urban landscapes are unevenly developed, ethnically and economically structured mosaics that concentrate poverty, hazard, risk, and protection. The sharp divisions in the urban landscape have actually deepened as the economy has globalized (Sassen 1994). This process of isolating poverty and concentrating risk, hazard, and protection produces place-based health effects. But inequality's effects on communities and societies cannot be so easily isolated in this landscape of "creative destruction." Wilkinson (1996) has shown that inequality is an affliction which may indeed infect whole societies' health. Using data on life expectancies and cause-specific mortality rates in a variety of countries, he demonstrates a positive relationship between income inequality and poor health at the societal level. Life expectancy is dramatically higher in countries where income inequality is modest and where social cohesion is high. Particularly among developed societies, it isn't the richest countries which have the best health, but rather the ones with a more egalitarian socioeconomic system. The lowest mortality rates for cancer, heart disease, infectious disease, as well as more socially related causes of death such as accidents, homicide, and addiction-related illnesses are found in more egalitarian societies. He reasons that such countries tend to have a stronger community life, and that the psychosocial support provided in these settings promotes health. It is thus not so much that economic growth has health benefits; rather, economic growth can improve life quality, which in turn has a health benefit. Thus life quality is more directly related to health. Place is a critical element in life quality. As both ethological and geographic writings suggest (see particularly Chapter 2) we are a place-orienting species by nature and culture. When expectations of place are thwarted or disappointed, stress and ill health are likely to develop.

The Homeless

As the economy has globalized, large sectors of the urban poor have become increasingly underemployed and the poorest have gotten even poorer. The marginalization of the poor, along with a steady rise in the cost of housing, coupled with a decline in the supply of low-income housing, have led to a situation in which a larger segment of the urban poor are at risk for becoming homeless (Wright, Rubin, and Devine 1998). Among the most susceptible to these risks are the poor who suffer from some form of health problem—those with addictions, chronic physical health problems, or mental illness. In a review of data for 16 Health Care for the Homeless Program sites with more than 63,000 clients, James Wright and associates Beth Rubin and Joel Devine (1998) note that health professionals cited alcohol and drug abuse as the primary factor in the homelessness of 32 percent of the client sample, and as a major factor in an additional 22 percent of cases. These care providers also listed chronic mental illness as the primary factor in the homelessness of 16 percent, and a major factor in an additional 18 percent; in contrast, poor physical health was the primary factor in only 3 percent of cases and a major factor in an additional 10 percent. Another risk factor associated with the incidence of homelessness is "doubling up," where an individual is taken in by someone else on a temporary basis. It is very often the step immediately prior to actual homelessness. This form of marginalized housing often leads to household crowding, which has been linked with marital dissension, psychological distress, and overt tension in parent-child relationships (Wright, Caspi, et al. 1998). The pathological nature of this form of home space (unclear territorial rights along with violations of basic spatial needs) tends to interact with the social, psychological, and physical vulnerabilities of those doubling up and increases their likelihood of homelessness. But the link between health and homelessness is much more complicated than a one-way causal relationship where poverty and health problems trigger homelessness.

The spatial deprivation of homelessness represents an extreme form of poverty. It is a unhealthy state—an inhuman condition because we are place-oriented by nature. Homelessness leaves basic place-based requirements unfulfilled. The homeless can make no claims to the spaces they occupy. While ethologists may claim that modern cultures emphasize a need for privacy, a modicum of personal space, access to places for social interaction, and safe and defensible spaces (see Chapter 2), these are not available to the homeless. Placelessness is both disorienting and demeaning. Physical or mental disorientation is seen as a symptom of illness. The disorienting condition of homelessness is clearly pathological, and, at the same time, debasing. Personal worth is socially and psychologically demonstrated by the place people can call their own. It follows that those who can literally call "no place" their own are socially and psychologically devalued or, perhaps more accurately, viewed as without value.

While place matters, being without place matters most to human beings. We spend our entire lives struggling to find "our place" in society, in history, and in the cosmic order; the link between place and identity is basic. It is not surprising, then, that when homeless persons are asked about their single most important possession, the majority list things connected directly with their identity—identification cards, official papers, or personal and family photographs—rather than more instrumental objects such as money, clothing, travel bags, or weapons (LaGory, Ritchey, Mullis et al. 1987). In a personal world without territory, nothing becomes more critical or basic than establishing one's place in society.

Homelessness is fundamentally dehumanizing. It is also a vivid reminder of both our own vulnerability (the old saw of "just a paycheck away") and of capitalism's propensity toward creative destruction. Homelessness looms large in the public conscience. While the structure of the metropolis is such that most residents can usually ignore the landscapes of creative destruction by carefully choosing commuting routes and by segregating residentially, it is much harder to avoid encounters with the homeless in daily routines. They are a distinctly visible group of urban poor. It is estimated that nearly 70 percent of urban Americans see the homeless in the course of their daily routine, and this visibility has been increasing since the 1980s (Blau 1992). These encounters, however, can provide only a glimpse into the pathological nature of placelessness.

To be without home is to be deprived of the very spaces that provide for and honor human needs. It is more than an absence of shelter or a severe form of poverty: it is a life filled with overwhelming daily hassles. And because the homeless life conflicts with basic human needs, it is by nature stress-filled. This comes across vividly in the following description of one part of the homeless experience:

> You're tired, you're hungry, you stink, and you're in there with a bunch of people you don't know and they're tired and they stink. I don't care who you are, you could stand your own feet and your own farts, but sometimes guys puke on themselves, or they shit on themselves. And you're in there trying to make it—you're trying to save your money. . . . It'll get to you and you'll think, "God, I need a drink. I need to get outta here. I need to get high." Try to lay down and you gotta get up the next day and go to work. Can't sleep. Can't rest. You'd rather go out and sleep on the street, but you're afraid of what's out there. (Snow and Anderson 1993:73)

While these words graphically depict the pathological condition of shelter life, there is far more to a homeless person's day and night than this portrait captures. Homelessness is severe poverty, with the added deprivation of placelessness. This deprivation means more than a personal absence of income and resources, more than living in the context of others' poverty. It denotes a total denial of spatial needs. What is life like without place?

It means struggling in a shadowy, hazard-filled world where at least temporarily there is no place of your own. In such a world, the most relevant question for the homeless is not who owns the property or whether it is public or private land, but rather whether the community's domiciled population views the property you are occupying as important. When a place has little value to housed citizens (abandoned buildings, vacant lots, skid rows, underpasses, etc.) the homeless can use it as a temporary place to live (Snow and Anderson 1993). These marginal places are often ceded to the propertyless, yet such spaces are impermanent territory, for occupants have no legal right to them. Marginal space can be quickly redefined by various groups as the public's space. Despite their impermanence such places at least offer a modicum of respite from placelessness. These spaces, however, are gradually shrinking in cities where urban renewal, revitalization, and gentrification have reshaped the urban area (Hoch and Slayton 1989; Snow and Anderson 1993).

Just as urban space has decentralized, so have the places that the homeless require for daily survival. Services offered in the highly centralized areas of skid row have now dispersed. As a result, homeless people often spend a lot of their day moving around to get services, to socialize, or to be alone. They spend much of their time in public space, which makes them more visible and thus more subject to surveillance and control. In these circumstances, visibility also makes their stigmatized identity more personally difficult to manage and control. They are constantly reminded by pedestrians' glances of pity or disapproval, or by the words and gestures of business owners and police, that they are out of place here. Yet there is often no "there" where this sense of being-out-of-place can fully disappear. As such, homelessness deteriorates critical psychological resources—self-esteem and the sense of mastery—which have been shown to mediate depression and physical health problems in the face of stressful circumstances (LaGory et al. 1990).

The daily difficulties of homelessness include more than challenges to identity and esteem. Homelessness is a life with significant risks and exposure to hazards; its incidence is typically preceded or accompanied by multiple life crises. The most common reasons given for homelessness are problems with personal relations (divorce, separation, domestic violence, problems getting along with others in the household), finances, or substance abuse by the person or a significant other (LaGory, Ritchey, and Gerald 1995). But that "presenting" problem is typically one in a longer list of negative life events experienced by the homeless person. The homeless episode often is preceded by negative events in childhood. Several studies indicate that persons who report unhappy childhoods, sexual or physical abuse, or unusual housing arrangements during childhood tend to have a higher prevalence of homelessness and a longer duration of homeless episodes (LaGory et al. 1995; Piliavin et al. 1993). This negative life history may create a degree of vulnerability to health risks and hazards that can be exacerbated by the dangerous environs and the limited environmental control exhibited by the homeless. In addition, people exposed to such negative circumstances and events may be more likely to take risks that further debilitate their already weakened physical and mental health.

Risk and Hazard among the Homeless

This mixture of dangerous circumstances, psychologically debilitating experiences, and a high propensity for risk taking have dramatic health consequences for the homeless. These risks and hazards result in a significantly higher rate of infectious diseases, chronically debilitating illnesses, and criminal victimization than for the general population. For that matter, the health problems of the homeless go well beyond those of other impoverished groups (Wright, Rubin, and Devine 1998). A study by Ropers and Boyer (1987) of homeless in Los Angeles showed that the proportion of homeless reporting themselves to be in "poor health" was 70 percent higher than for the very poor who were housed. Brickner et al. (1985) succinctly state the health challenges facing the homeless:

> [T]he medical disorders of the homeless are all the ills to which the flesh is heir, magnified by disordered living conditions, exposure to extremes of heat and cold, lack of protection from rain and snow, bizarre sleeping accommodations and overcrowding in shelters. These factors are exacerbated by stress, psychiatric disorders and sociopathic behavior patterns. (p. 3)

In order to explore these unique health challenges we first examine the risks and hazards associated with homelessness and then explore specific health outcomes. Finally, we look at the role of psychosocial resources in inoculating the homeless against such circumstances. The hazards of living in public space's interstices are many. Homeless environments are less predictable and controllable. Among the everyday hassles confronted by the homeless are problems with noise, privacy, overcrowding, theft, safety, and access to basic resources such as food, toilets, and clothing.

Not only do the homeless live on the margins where space can be easily reclaimed by force or threat of force, but the spaces they occupy tend to be nonresidential in character, posing unique dangers to those in residence there. Living in these spaces increases exposure to the hazards of weather, chemical and noise pollution, unsafe building materials, dilapidated structures, combustible materials, poor ventilation, vehicular and pedestrian traffic, and vermin. Indeed, the so-called "street homeless" are officially defined as residing in spaces not meant for human habitation, such as "streets, parks, alleys, parking ramps, parts of the highway system, transportation depots and other parts of the transportation systems (e.g., subway tunnels, railway cars), all-night commercial establishments (e.g., movie theaters, laundromats, restaurants), abandoned buildings, squatter situations, building roofs or stairwells, chicken coops and other farm outbuildings, caves, campgrounds, vehicles and other similar places" (Burt 1992:3). These spaces are literally hazardous to the health of those who spend significant parts of their day and night within them. It's not surprising, then, that homeless people generally say that it has been much harder for them to stay healthy since becoming homeless (LaGory et al. 1995).

Those who spend most of their time in shelters avoid some of the physical hazards associated with street life, but encounter a completely different set of challenges. Large numbers of persons in relatively poor health sleep together in dormitory-style settings with mats or cots only a few inches from each other. They share communal showers, toilets, and dining facilities. The high-density shelter setting promotes the transmission of infectious and communicable diseases ranging from minor disorders (colds and flu) to potentially fatal illnesses such as tuberculosis (Wright 1989). Overcrowding is also a psychologically distressing circumstance that can lead to poor mental health and strained social relations. It can accelerate personal conflicts that carry over into other settings, promoting aggression and fighting. James Wright (1989) reports that a significant number of the injuries treated by the Health Care for the Homeless Program were for injuries sustained in altercations between shelter residents.

Homeless people dwell in a socially predatory environment, where security and defense is a constant concern. Living in public spaces, even on the margin, exposes people to the risks of intrusion, creating a sense of defenselessness and insecurity. Those living on the street often compensate for this lack of security by adopting a militarylike strategy in which individuals take shifts watching for intruders during sleeping hours. It is hard to feel at home when, during sleeping hours, circumstances are more like a battlefield than a home. Almost all homeless persons characterize the streets as dangerous, particularly at night (Fitzpatrick, LaGory, and Ritchey 1993). Criminologists argue that the convergence in time and space of *suitable targets, motivated offenders,* and the *absence of capable guardians* increases the probability of predatory offenses such as robbery and assault (Cohen and Felson 1979). These three conditions are present on the street. Not surprisingly then, victimization rates are unusually high among the homeless (Fitzpatrick et al. 1993; Snow and Anderson 1993).

In a 1995 study of homeless in Birmingham, Alabama, 22 percent of respondents had been robbed in the six months prior to being interviewed. Thirty-four percent of those victims had been mugged or beaten up during the robbery (LaGory et al. 1995). When robberies were excluded from victimization episodes, 14 percent had been attacked with a knife, and 57 percent with a gun. These rates of victimization are dramatically higher than those for the general population. For example, the robbery rate was six per thousand annually in the general population (Bureau of Justice Statistics 1992), but 220 per thousand for homeless respondents in a six-month period (LaGory et al. 1995). Additionally, there were four times more rapes and nearly six times more assaults among the homeless over six months as compared to the general population over the course of a year. A majority of homeless crime victims were victims of violent crimes. While some of the victimization rates could be attributable to poverty, research shows that rates of all types of victimization were considerably higher for the homeless than for other low-income groups (Fitzpatrick et al. 1993; Wright, Rubin, and Devine 1998).

Even if a homeless person escaped being a crime victim, chances were slim that he or she had escaped seeing a crime committed (LaGory et al. 1995). In the same study city, one-third of the homeless had witnessed a physical attack in the previous six months; more than one-fourth had seen someone else knifed or shot. Because of exposure to these violent circumstances, more than one-third carried a gun or knife for protection. While the homeless who commit crimes often victimize other homeless people (Snow and Anderson 1993), predation is not common.

Indeed, the rule of behavior appears to be "what goes around comes around." While trust is eroded by the conditions of the street, even under these most dire of circumstances, a social organization emerges. Nevertheless, exposure to strangers and to dangerous circumstances makes life more unpredictable and stressful.

There are established routines to everyday life among groups of homeless people, but these routines often add to the hazards and risks associated with homelessness (Snow and Anderson 1993). To carve out some degree of independence on the margins requires a modest but fairly steady income. Homeless incomes, however, are extremely low—the median monthly income for homeless individuals in the Birmingham metropolitan area, for example, was $275 per month (LaGory et al. 1995). Income typically is derived from one or more of four sources— wage labor, shadow work, family support networks, and formal programs. Only a small portion (less than 20 percent) of the homeless population receives money from a pension or from federal or state transfer payment programs (LaGory et al. 1995; Snow and Anderson 1993). While some may receive money from family members, in most cases this support is meager and erratic.

The vast majority of homeless get their income from wage labor or shadow work. Because of their limited skills, however, the wage labor is almost exclusively low-skill day labor at or near the minimum wage. This work is physically taxing, sometimes dangerous, and its availability is highly variable. The significant physical and mental health problems of the homeless, their limited skill levels, along with the unpredictable supply of work, makes even a modest labor income uncertain. Unconventional means of gaining income, so-called shadow work, is thus often relied upon. Such "work" includes selling and trading (personal possessions, illegal goods and services, and plasma), panhandling, scavenging, and stealing. It often has significant health risks attached to it. Thus, the most often used sources of income available, day labor and shadow work, not only provide meager and unpredictable income streams, but often expose the worker to hazardous circumstances and require risk-taking behaviors that further threaten health.

The risky circumstances of the homeless include exposure to violence, unsafe work conditions, marginal spaces, unpredictable environments, harmful chemicals and pollutants, and contagion. In addition, health risks are further exacerbated by the stress of a life situation which by its very nature frustrates basic physical, psychological, and social needs. These unsafe and stressful circumstances are sometimes accompanied by risk-taking behaviors which may be an additional factor in the health of the homeless. Homelessness appears to be associated with risk-taking behaviors such as binge drinking, drug abuse, risky sexual practices, and weapons possession (LaGory et al. 1995; Snow and Anderson 1993; Wright, Rubin, and Devine 1998). In one study of the homeless, 23 percent were binge drinkers, 12 percent were currently using drugs, 3 percent shared needles, and although nearly half reported having multiple sexual partners, only 30 percent of those sexually active said they ever used a condom (LaGory et al. 1995). While risk taking may actually be a factor in the incidence of homelessness among some persons, for others it is an outcome of being on the streets. Whatever its reasons, those who engage in risk-taking behavior further exacerbate the health-compromising circumstances of homelessness.

Health among the Homeless

Homelessness is a pathological state that promotes illness. A number of studies highlight the severe physical and mental health problems faced by the homeless (Burt and Cohen 1989; Rossi et al. 1986; Wright, Rubin, and Devine 1998). Notwithstanding the fact that health problems may be implicated in the incidence of homelessness (alcohol or drug addiction, chronic mental illness, etc.), the homeless condition itself is a source of poor health. Placelessness is a fundamentally distressing circumstance —a chronic stressor. Much research demonstrates that severe stress can trigger significant mental health problems as well as genetic predispositions to certain physical disorders such as hypertension (Lin et al. 1986; Wright, Rubin, and Devine 1998). The physical circumstances of homelessness (crowding, dangerous sleeping sites, poor diets) also increase the chances of contracting chronic and infectious disorders.

The most comprehensive and reliable source of information on the health of the homeless comes from the Health Care for the Homeless Programs (Wright 1989; Wright, Rubin, and Devine 1998). Analysis of these data suggests striking disparities between the physical and mental health of the homeless and others. The most prevalent acute physical disorders among the homeless are upper respiratory infections, traumas, and various minor and major skin ailments. Each of these disorders exhibits a prevalence rate three to six times higher than the general urban population. For chronic physical disorders, the most common conditions are hypertension, arthritis and other musculoskeletal disorders, dental problems, gastrointestinal ailments, peripheral vascular disease, neurological disorders, eye disease, genitourinary problems, ear disorders, and chronic obstructive pulmonary disease. Stress-related illnesses such as hypertension and gastrointestinal disorders are prevalent among the homeless. Hypertension is two to four times higher, while gastrointestinal disorders (ranging from ulcers and hernias to diarrhea and gastritis) are two to three times greater. Peripheral vascular disease (leading to edema, thromboses, cellulitis, ulceration, and in some cases, gangrene) is four to five times more prevalent. The high prevalence of this disease is attributable to the spatial circumstances of the homeless lifestyle (constant forced walking, exposure to the elements, cramped sleeping arrangements, and poor hygiene).

James Wright and his colleagues (Wright, Rubin, and Devine 1998) point out that unlike most sick people, the sick homeless are not usually isolated from the healthy, resulting in the likely spread of infectious and communicable disease among the homeless and a potential threat to the public health. Of greatest concern are the rates for AIDS and tuberculosis infection. The prevalence of AIDS cases among the homeless is more than 10 times that of the homed, while the rate of tuberculosis among the homeless is 100 times higher. Tuberculosis steadily declined in the general population from the 1950s to the early 1980s, when the rate of decline leveled off, with new antibiotic-resistant strains appearing. Some researchers believe that it is no coincidence that this trend coincided with the upsurge in homelessness during the 1980s (Wright, Rubin, and Devine 1998).

National estimates suggest that approximately 30 percent of the homeless suffer from severe chronic mental illness (LaGory et al. 1995; Snow and Anderson 1993; Wright, Rubin, Devine 1998). In many cases, mental illness is one component of a dual diagnosis of substance abuse and mental disorder. For example, studies in Birmingham showed that 14 percent had been diagnosed or treated for severe mental illness only, while an additional 16 percent had a diagnosable mental illness along with a substance abuse problem (LaGory et al. 1995). This comorbidity indicates a complexity of health and behavioral problems that makes treatment exceptionally difficult. Nevertheless, all major studies seem to agree that while mental illness is a significant problem for the homeless, the majority do not have a severe mental health condition (LaGory et al. 1995; Snow and Anderson 1993; Wright, Rubin, Devine 1998). Stories in the media, however, continue to interpret the homeless crisis as a direct result of changing mental health policies. It is very clear from all available data that the two-decade upsurge in homelessness is not the result of a shift toward the community mental health philosophy that encouraged deinstitutionalization. The deinstitutionalized mentally ill represent a minor segment of the homeless population. Snow and Anderson (1993), for example, traced mental health records of a sample of homeless in Austin, Texas, and discovered that only 11 percent had ever been hospitalized for a psychiatric disorder. Indeed, research suggests that among the mentally ill homeless, the majority have never been institutionalized (Wright, Rubin, Devine 1998). The real concern shouldn't be over the mentally ill homeless released inappropriately (deinstitutionalization), but rather over a failed system in which many never even get treated for their problem.

Perhaps the most prevalent mental health problem faced by the homeless is depression. It is estimated that as many as 80 percent of the homeless population show the symptoms of clinical depression (LaGory et al. 1990, 1995). Prevalence rates for depression are approximately seven times higher than among the homed population. Yet in most cases it would be inappropriate to designate this depressive symptomatology as mental illness. Indeed, it is more likely a normal psychological reaction to abnormal circumstances. Whatever its etiology (exogenous or endogenous), its prevalence suggests the level of suffering endemic to the condition of placelessness. Twenty-eight percent of the homeless have had suicidal thoughts since becoming homeless, and approximately 40 percent of those persons have actually attempted suicide during their homelessness (LaGory et al. 1995).

Psychosocial Protection against Hazards and Risks of Homelessness

The normal protective devices available to homed populations (informal and formal social supports and inner resources) are often significantly deteriorated by the homeless circumstance itself. These factors usually mediate the effects of stressors and serve to protect at-risk persons from some of the health problems typically associated with risky social and psychological circumstances. Homelessness dilutes the protective effect on health and mental health symptoms.

This is most notable in the formal support systems associated with health care. The homeless face profound barriers to health care access (Wright, Rubin, Devine 1998). These barriers are structured around three basic dimensions: the homeless circumstance itself, health behaviors and attitudes of the homeless, as well as deficiencies in medical service delivery systems. The circumstance of homelessness is so profoundly pathological, denying the most basic needs of food, shelter, clothing, and defense, that health problems are often a low-priority consideration. This is tragic given their significantly higher prevalence rates for many physical and mental health disorders. It also signals the potential for a much larger public health problem. A study of urban homeless in Los Angeles found that less than half of those reporting a chronic medical condition had seen a doctor in the last year, and only 13 percent had a regular physician whom they could see (Robertson and Cousineau 1986). The reason most often cited for not seeing a physician was cost—very few homeless (19 percent) had health insurance. Besides affordability, common rationales for not using health care services are skepticism about the seriousness of the problem, lack of transportation, being too sick to travel or walk to the service, distrust of doctors, conflicts with work, and lack of knowledge of available services (LaGory et al. 1995).

While the lack of resources associated with homelessness is a critical factor in health service utilization, it is much more than simply a poverty effect. The complex and distressing circumstances of homelessness may actually distract people from health concerns. At the same time, poor health itself may ironically impede service usage. Mobility-impairing illness, coupled with a lack of transportation, creates a friction of distance which is very difficult to overcome. The fact that homeless persons reside in marginal spaces sometimes promotes inaccessibility to health services since these spaces are often in unclaimed, undesirable locations where quality services are unlikely to exist. In addition, high levels of substance abuse and mental health disorders may promote distrust and fear of health providers. That is, lifestyle adaptations and risky behaviors associated with some segments of homeless such as alcohol and drug abuse, sleeping on the streets, and so on, may result in health beliefs and behaviors that discourage people to seek health care.

Another problem, however, lies in the health care delivery system itself. Wright, Rubin, and Devine (1998) suggest problems including an inadequate supply of public health care resources, lack of sufficient numbers of providers accepting low-income patients, lack of service locations near heavy concentrations of the homeless, and physician and administrator attitudes that often define the homeless patient as unworthy or undesirable. To transcend these problems, programs such as Health Care for the Homeless employ outreach programs that include rotating clinics at shelters and soup kitchens, as well as mobile units that regularly patrol the marginal spaces frequented by the homeless. Because urban ecology, particularly for the homeless, involves rather dramatic time-space fluctuation, these patrols often take place at night when individuals are more likely to be found at rest.

Health support is not just a function of a formal delivery system. Much evidence exists to show that health is dramatically affected by informal sources of support as well. Informal networks (family and friends) provide important caregiving services, useful information, and psychological support in times of physical and mental distress (LaGory et al. 1991; Lin et al. 1986; Umberson 1987). Despite earlier explanations of homelessness as the result of disaffiliation from such support, research in the last 20 years indicates the homeless to be affiliated (LaGory et al. 1991; Snow and Anderson 1993). They have networks of friends, relatives, and acquaintances that can be relied on for instrumental and expressive support. Indeed, fewer than 10 percent of the homeless people in the Birmingham study lacked social support or sustained contacts with acquaintances (LaGory et al.1991). Sixty percent had a close personal friend in the area, 70 percent visited relatives, and half had visited their parents during the last several months. These ties provided at least some tangible support: 70 percent received aid over the last year from relatives, and 63 percent got help from friends.

These networks, however, differed significantly from those in the general population. While a majority of urban adults are married, very few of the homeless are—7 percent in both the Birmingham (LaGory et al. 1995) and Chicago (Rossi 1989) studies. This partner bond is a critical strong tie mediating stress in the general population; its absence is undoubtedly consequential for the homeless. Other differences are notable between the homed and the homeless networks when results from a well-known study of general population networks (Wellman 1979) are compared with the Birmingham homeless network data (LaGory, Ritchey, and Mullis 1991). Ninety-eight percent of the general urban population had intimate or close friends, while only 79 percent of the homeless had close friends. Fifty percent of intimate ties in the general population are with relatives, while for the homeless relatives are an insignificant source. Finally, while the average number of intimate or close ties in the general population is five, the average homeless person has only three such ties.

That is not to say that informal support does not matter. Research shows that social support reduces depressive symptoms among the homeless (LaGory et al. 1990; Schutt, Meschede, and Rierdan 1994). Distress itself is known to have a significant impact on health and well-being, but these effects appear mixed for the homeless (LaGory et al. 1991). Particularly striking is the fact that homeless persons with social support still describe their lives as lonely. One clear reason for this is that homelessness is such a stigmatized condition that it produces a sense of separation from normal society not easily overcome by social attachment. Obviously, the ecology of homelessness reinforces this marginalization. In addition, the severe multiple life stressors of a homeless circumstance are so debilitating that even significant informal social ties may not be capable of overcoming them. Exchange theory (Emerson 1972) suggests that the imbalanced exchanges found in homeless networks cannot be sustained for long periods of time. The homeless person's support system is unlikely to have resources substantial enough to assist with their extensive needs (most friends and relatives will themselves likely be poor).

In addition to formal and informal social support, the inner resources of the individual also have been shown to play an important role in health (Lin et al. 1986). Persons who display a sense of mastery over external circumstances (inner locus of control or mastery) respond to stressful circumstances in much healthier ways than those who see the world fatalistically (Pearlin and Schooler 1978). For the homeless, mastery has a very significant role in mediating distress and reducing depressive symptoms (LaGory et al. 1990). Recent research on religion and spirituality suggests their potential importance in responding to stressful circumstances (Idler and Kasl 1992). Thus it is not surprising to note that homeless score high on standard measures of spirituality (LaGory et al. 1995). While the impact of religion and spirituality on the health of the homeless is not yet clear, it appears that those with high levels of spirituality are more likely to seek out services for health problems (LaGory et al. 1995). This appears to be more true of people with addiction problems.

Some homeless advocates portray homelessness as a significant spiritual and moral challenge facing communities. It signifies that something is very wrong in those communities where it continues to be a significant problem. It is a dehumanizing condition that strips the individual of basic human dignities. A society or community that tolerates these circumstances must surely come to grips with the contradiction between basic moral principles and the structural conditions that produce such circumstances. The spiritual dilemma that confronts such communities and societies is an intriguing issue for an ecology of health, but even more interesting is that the homeless often display deeper spirituality than the homed (LaGory et al. 1995). The fact of high spirituality among the homeless seems to contradict Maslow's hierarchy of needs (1954). The homeless, who find themselves literally without spaces in a world in which place matters greatly, must carve out a "place" in a world of leftover spaces. The sense of placelessness which is engendered, however, is to a degree mollified by carving out and honing interior space. Not even the homeless can be said to be truly placeless. Yet this interiorization of space certainly cannot compensate for the spatial indignities and injustices of a homeless life—a life that severely wounds its victims both physically and psychologically.

While homelessness represents an extreme form of poverty and a unique ecological circumstance with unprecedented consequences for health, it is also a far less prevalent expression of poverty than that found in the ghettos of America's cities. Approximately 500,000 to 700,000 people are homeless on any given day (Wright, Rubin, and Devine 1998). While that number is high, poverty among minority groups is a much more common problem. More than 26 percent of African-American and Hispanic households fall below the poverty line

(U.S. Bureau of the Census 1998). For African Americans alone, this is a population of approximately 9 million poor persons. A significant portion of this group of minority poor live in ghetto communities where this poverty is further compounded by segregation. The subject of minority poverty, particularly ghettoized minority poverty, and its health consequences is explored in the rest of this chapter.

Racial and Ethnic Minorities

Decades after the civil rights movement, America remains a nation divided as it continues to confront disturbing inequities between Whites and nonwhites. At the heart of this division is a segregated society that perpetuates the barriers between rich and poor, White and nonwhite. Thus where we live in the metropolis is a function of the interrelationship between race and class, with residential location accentuating just how disparate some groups are. For example, we know that Blacks are more likely to get sick, stay sick longer, and die prematurely compared to Whites (Andrulis 1997; Hummer 1996). While other racial and ethnic minorities face similar disparities, empirical evidence suggests that health risk, mortality, disease and illness, and access to health care are of particular concern for African Americans (Davis 1991; Dressler 1993; Geiger 1992; LeClere et al. 1997; Williams 1996). Nearly 25 years ago, the Kerner Commission warned that America was heading toward the creation of "two societies—one black, one White—separate and unequal" (U.S. National Advisory Commission on Civil Disorders 1968). This vision of the future has become a nightmarish reality for some as we move into the new millennium.

As suggested in earlier parts of the book, health outcomes are a function of the complicated interrelationship between place, status, behavior, and social structure. While our intention has been to try to isolate this "place effect," other aspects of the relationship need to be considered. In particular, this part of the chapter focuses on the interaction between status and place and its commanding role in determining negative health outcomes for at-risk populations such as low-income minorities. Indeed, the most compelling explanation for the severity of their experiences relative to other groups is their high concentration in areas undergoing the most severe economic and social decline—the inner cities. This concentration of poverty affects not only the social and economic health of America's central cities but also creates an underclass that slips further and further from the American dream. With more than 3,000 high-poverty neighborhoods in the United States containing nearly 9 million residents, these places and their potential negative effects on residents' physical and mental health are much too common an occurrence for such a wealthy nation as the United States.

Theories of the Underclass

Contemporary urban scholars argue that an urban underclass, consisting largely of poor African Americans and other minority groups, is becoming a permanent feature of the American urban landscape (Jargowsky 1997; Massey and Denton 1993; Wilson 1987, 1996). This group has generally been cut off from social and economic opportunities for growth and success. They are isolated within specific neighborhoods in the metropolitan area—powerless, marginalized, and unable to escape from poverty given their economic and educational deficiencies. How this underclass originated is of some debate, yet its role in helping shape the character of the inner city seems clear. As low-income minorities have become increasingly concentrated in narrowly defined geographic areas, the level of poverty has been compounded and reinforced by a host of other problems, including high rates of crime, drug use, delinquency, teenage pregnancy, and welfare dependency. This cyclical process has further contributed to the demise of many urban neighborhoods, leaving their residents disconnected and underserved by the urban resource machine.

The truth of this characterization is confirmed in the neighborhoods bordering Village Creek. As we discussed earlier, many residents continue to struggle with the environmental threats (pollution and flooding) posed by the creek as well as the weakened economic and social structure of the neighborhoods they live in. From the eastern side of Birmingham originating in the Airport Hills neighborhood, Village Creek winds through or passes under 26 census tracts. Not all of these neighborhoods are harmed equally by the creek. Rather, three neighborhoods are exposed to flooding and its concomitant health risks. These places typify what contemporary urban scholars refer to as "underclass" neighborhoods that have become home to the new urban poor (Jargowsky 1997; Massey and Denton 1993; Wilson 1987, 1996). Jargowsky (1997), through a combination of fieldwork and review of prior community classifications (e.g., Wilson 1987), operationalizes the underclass (ghetto) neighborhood as predominantly Black with at least 40 percent of the total households living below the poverty level. Interestingly, all three of the census tracts identified as "problem tracts" regarding their exposure to Village Creek meet the criterion for an underclass/ghetto neighborhood. In addition to their percentage of Black residents (99 percent) and percentage of households living below the poverty level (42 percent), these three Birmingham neighborhoods meet other national underclass criteria: median household income ($11,338), the percentage of vacant housing units (18 percent), percentage of female-headed families with children (39 percent), and median home value ($31,000).

How these three neighborhoods got to this point in their development continues to be the subject of some discussion. During the 1980s, several works attempted to describe the evolution of the urban underclass. Douglas Glasgow (1980) argued in his book *The Black Underclass* that the likely and most persistent cause of the underclass was racism. By suggesting that American institutions (education, religion, economic, government) failed to address the comprehensive needs of Blacks, he argued that institutional practices motivated by racism established Black poverty and perpetuated an underclass position for Blacks. Others joined the debate and suggested that Black poverty, instead of being motivated by racism, was actually the product of a welfare system that created dependencies. This conservative argument suggested that welfare benefits were too generous and too permissive—thus making it "profitable" for the poor to use welfare as a means of sustenance and lowered obligation (Mead 1986; Murray 1984).

William Julius Wilson attacked these conservative characterizations of the American welfare state in his 1987 book *The Truly Disadvantaged.* He argued that the urban poor were not in their predicament because of an overly generous or too permissive welfare system. Rather, he proposed that it was geographic, social, and economic isolation that prohibited Blacks' advancement in a system where one's success depended on how connected residents and their neighborhoods were to the larger metropolitan resource machine (Massey and Denton 1993). The steady outmigration of working- and middle-class Blacks created a structural transformation in inner city neighborhoods that were once economically vibrant, turning them into socially and economically stagnant ghettos.

While these arguments were convincing, what was missing from the discussion of the underlying causes of urban poverty was an elaboration of the role of racial segregation in the production of poverty. Massey and Denton (1993) in their seminal work, *American Apartheid,* argue their position in the following excerpt:

> Geographically concentrated poverty is built into the experience of urban blacks by racial segregation. Segregation, not middle-class out-migration, is the key factor responsible for the creation and perpetuation of communities characterized by persistent and spatially concentrated poverty. . . . The coincidence of rising poverty and high levels of segregation guarantees that blacks will be exposed to a social and economic environment that is far harsher than anything experienced by any other racial or ethnic group. (p. 118)

Racial segregation is seen as crucial to both identifying and understanding the urban underclass. The process of segregation helps to explain why the urban underclass consists primarily of Blacks and Puerto Ricans—these are the two groups that most often have experienced increases in poverty and residential segregation simultaneously (Massey and Denton 1993). In addition, they argue that the majority of these underclass communities are located in older metropolitan areas of the Northeast and Midwest—regions of the country that experienced significant economic decline and increasing levels of racial segregation beginning in the early 1970s. Evidence seems to point to a recurring theme—in order to address the problems of poverty we must first address the problem of racial segregation.

Clearly, increasing concentrations of poverty have been intimately connected to increasing concentrations of certain racial groups in specific areas of the metropolis. The high correlation between these two has created an ecology of inequality that continues to have significant physical and mental health implications for its residents. This ecology creates an unstable and unattractive social environment that may be not only a force in the spread of such diseases as AIDS, but also a barrier to developing and implementing new strategies for health promotion and disease prevention. In his presidential address to the Population Association of America, Douglas Massey (1996) sums up this powerful role that an ecology of inequality plays in determining the future of American cities:

> Just as poverty is concentrated spatially, anything correlated with poverty is also concentrated. Therefore, as the density of poverty increases in cities throughout the world, so will the density of joblessness, crime, family dissolution, drug abuse, alcoholism, disease, and violence. Not only will the poor have to grapple with the manifold problems due to their own lack of income; increasingly they also will have to confront the social effects of living in an environment where most of the neighbors are also poor. At the same time, the concentration of affluence will create a social environment for the rich that is opposite in every respect from that of the poor. (p. 407)

This in fact is the very problem that faces neighborhoods bordering Village Creek. These places have become residential "hazard zones," where the concentration of risk is so great making it especially difficult for place-bound, at-risk groups such as the elderly, youth, and minorities, to stay healthy. In addition, it complicates service delivery and intervention strategies that attempt to address multiple problems among a variety of subgroups in a single neighborhood or catchment area.

Ethnic Enclaves

Ethnic enclave theory runs somewhat contrary to the underclass assumptions concerning the health and welfare of segregated, low-income minority groups. This particular assimilation argument suggests that under special social and economic circumstances minorities may actually benefit from isolation and segregation from the majority (Bonacich and Modell 1980; Portes and Bach 1985; Portes and Zhou 1996; Wilson and Portes 1980). Much of the early literature on the ethnic economy/enclave focused on the Asian immigrant experience. Studies examined the role of Chinese and Japanese ethnic economies in providing employment, business opportunity, and potential success for minorities that faced hostility and institutional racism (Alba and Nee

1997). Even in the face of such racism, small businesses and employment opportunities created alternative sources of income and provided a means of survival for many immigrants. This unique form of adaptation to the structural barriers erected by the larger society have created ethnic immigrant communities that traditionally have provided care and support for its residents, but that support has not been risk- or cost-free for the immigrant.

As assimilated second and third generations abandon the enclave and look for employment and business opportunities, the enclave itself becomes challenged as a viable economy that may no longer be serving the needs of its residents. With limited capital and a tightly controlled market, growth and entrepreneurship become constrained; as the general U.S. economy continues to improve and opportunities increase for minorities, the enclave's role as a self-contained society is questioned. While the enclave serves important functions, particularly to new immigrants with limited knowledge of American society and a lack of proficiency in English, the by-product of increasing levels of geographic concentration threatens to impede the successful assimilation of immigrants into the larger society while limiting their health opportunities. Many of the ethnic enclaves traditionally were viewed as institutionally complete. However, in recent years that completeness has been altered by significant changes in the general economy, the delivery of medical services, and outreach programs designed to address health promotion and disease prevention in low-income minority communities.

As we consider the health implications of segregated racial and ethnic communities, we are again reminded of the significance of place. Surprisingly, much of the empirical research on health differences across racial and ethnic groups never attempts a systematic examination of the effects on the neighborhood or community and their role in determining physical or mental health outcomes. Instead, a great deal of work highlights sociodemographic, socioeconomic, and familial effects on mortality and illness rate differences among specific racial and ethnic groups (Adler et al. 1994; Pappas et al. 1993; Rogers 1992; Ross and Wu 1995; Sorlie, Backlund, and Keller 1995). These studies suggest that because some ethnic groups are more likely to have a disproportionate number of individuals who are less educated, divorced, and of lower socioeconomic status, they will have higher rates of illness and mortality. Thus, health outcomes are viewed as compositional. If we examine only demo-graphic differences, African Americans have higher mortality rates than Whites (Rogers 1992). However, several studies demonstrate that even when you control for individual-level differences between racial groups, the relative risk of disease and death for African Americans remains 30 to 60 percent higher than that of Whites (Sorlie et al. 1995). Research on Hispanics indicates a similar contradiction—compositional differences account for some of the health differences between Hispanics and non-Hispanics. Despite the demonstrated disadvantage, however, the expla-nation of these differences is incomplete (LeClere et al. 1997; Markides and Coreil 1986; Sorlie et al. 1993).

Context and Health Differences

Based on earlier discussions, we know that racial and ethnic minorities are not randomly distributed in metropolitan areas. Rather, these groups are steered into a small number of neighborhoods characterized as high-risk places with poverty, crime, and illness occurring indepen-dently of any individual differences in socioeconomic status (LeClere et al. 1997). Several studies, while acknowledging that individual differ-ences account for some of the variation in mortality between racial groups, demonstrate that community-level effects are important. Using data on a county in California, Haan and associates (Haan, Kaplan, and Camacho 1987) found that both African Americans and Whites living in a high-poverty area experienced higher mortality rates than those living in nonpoor areas. Whites in high-poverty areas experienced almost 50 percent higher mortality than Whites in nonpoor areas, and when neigh-borhood poverty is controlled, the ethnic gap in mortality is reduced by nearly 25 percent. Their argument is that some ethnic groups experience higher mortality because of where they live rather than just their ethnic-ity. Other recent studies confirm this earlier work, and suggest that mor-tality analyses are misspecified if they do not include both individual and contextual factors in the model (Rogers 1992; Sorlie et al. 1995). Places with low income and high concentrations of African Americans increase the likelihood of death for residents. Just as Jargowsky (1997) argues, these underclass neighborhoods are hazard zones where concentrated "deprivation can do irreparable harm."

When illness and disease are examined the results are similar. The rates of morbidity mirror mortality, and while individual differences (health behavior, beliefs, attitudes, etc.) account for some of the gap existing between Whites and racial and ethnic minorities, the characteristics of the communities that minorities live in account for much of this difference. Though researchers have shown for decades that ecological factors play a significant role in determining physical and mental health, public health policy continues to ignore the power of the community in influencing healthy outcomes.

Health in the 'Hood

In 1900, the life expectancy at birth in the United States was 47.6 years for Whites and 33 years for nonwhites (most of whom were Black). By the close of the twentieth-century, life expectancy for Whites has increased to 76 years and 69 years for Blacks (National Center for Health Statistics 1993). While progress has been made in improving the health status of both races, Blacks continue to bear the burden of premature death, excessive illness, and disability (Williams, Lavizzo-Mourey, and Warren 1994). While a substantial literature documents the role of individual-level factors in predicting negative health outcomes, the differential quality of the physical environment that Blacks and Whites live in clearly plays a deciding role in shaping health and mortality. A majority of African Americans live in large, urban, segregated cities where there is a high concentration of poverty (Massey and Denton 1993). These segregated cities concentrate hazard. Toxic environments, high-density dwellings and neighborhoods, vacant and substandard housing, high crime and dangerous living conditions all combine in a lethal way to create hazard zones for populations already at risk. With limited support, risky lifestyles, and institutional forces that interfere with the delivery of health services, it is no wonder then that African Americans are the highest health risk group in the country.

While these problems are amplified among the Black population they are not confined to Blacks. Deaths related to heart disease, cancer, and diabetes, as well as infant mortality, tend to be higher among Hispanics, Cubans, Native Americans, and even some subgroups of Asian and Pacific Islanders (U.S. Department of Health and Human Services 1985). Additionally, Hispanics and Latinos face unique health challenges. Latinos' risk of measles is three times higher than that of Black children, and fewer than 50 percent of Latino infants are immunized by the age of two (Mendoza 1994). Latinos' rates for homicide, AIDS infection, and STDs have increased, while drug and alcohol use continues to climb, and in some cases, outdistance their Black counterparts (Coalition of Hispanic Health and Human Organizations 1991; Mendoza 1994).

Though these health disparities are often explained statistically by individual-level variations in the composition of the populations, place matters. The population's location determines its exposure to risks in the physical environment as well as its access to resources that could be used to improve health (Williams 1990). Countless studies reinforce the notion that these differences in disease and death among racial and ethnic groups can be explained by individual-level variables (e.g., Feinstein 1993; Hummer 1996). Yet what is missing from many of these studies is more careful analysis of the role of place in producing physical and mental symptomatology among its residents. For example, while it is well documented that city life is generally more stressful than suburban life, not everyone living in the city is exposed equally to the high stress of the urban environment (Milgram 1972; Smith 1988; Srole et al. 1962). In neighborhoods where exposure to crime and violence is high, stress and secondary physical health problems are likely to be higher than in other central-city neighborhoods where crime and violence are not prevalent (Garbarino et al. 1992). It is well known that living in a socioeconomically depressed area with high exposure to poverty and racism may be particularly stress inducing (Kessler and Neighbors 1986). Some research indicates that even when controlling for socioeconomic differences, Blacks experience more stressful life events than Whites; racial and ethnic minorities still have higher rates of exposure to pollution, toxic poisoning, and other physical hazards (Bullard 1990; Bullard and Wright 1987). The impact of stress has also been associated with a variety of health problems including poor pregnancy outcomes (Hobel 1991), elevated blood pressure and diabetes (Cottington et al. 1985), and cancer and heart disease (Dodge and Martin 1979).

By paying more attention to the local geography and less to individual population differences, traditional explanations give way to more innovative ones. For example, Geronimus (1992) proposed a "weathering hypothesis" as a possible explanation for patterns of high morbidity and infant mortality among Blacks. Focusing on the hostility of the environment within which people live and work, she suggests that as exposure to environmental assaults and deficits increases with age, there is a worsening health status. A similar finding emerges in a recent study on the ethnic and socioeconomic factors that contribute to risk in cardiovascular heart disease (Winkelby et al.1998). The study finds significant differences in health risks (blood pressure, smoking, etc.) between Whites and racial/ethnic minorities, particularly Mexican Americans and African Americans. The authors argue for exploring alternative causal pathways and suggest that different life experiences as well as economic, time, and most important, residential constraints may be competing with healthy behaviors to further increase the risk of heart disease among minorities.

Village Creek Profile

Exposure to pollution and other social and environmental hazards has certainly been the Village Creek experience. These risky neighborhoods, fitting the criteria for inner-city areas (poor or underclass minority neighborhoods) confront a multitude of mental and physical ills linked to the spatial pattern of the metropolis. As noted earlier, three census tracts bordering Village Creek are classified as underclass, high-poverty minority neighborhoods. These tracts are in Jefferson County, the core county in the four-county Birmingham Metropolitan Statistical Area. With more than 650,000 residents, Jefferson is the largest county in the state of Alabama. The Village Creek segment of Jefferson County consists of 13,850 residents (2 percent of Jefferson County) and represents a little more than 5 percent of the city of Birmingham, which has a total population of approximately 270,000 persons. The racial composition of Jefferson County is 65 percent White and 35 percent nonwhite. In contrast to Jefferson County as a whole and to the remainder of the census tracts in the city of Birmingham, these three census tracts are nearly 99 percent nonwhite, predominantly African American (U.S. Bureau of the Census 1993).

Table 6.1 combines racial composition with other sociodemographic characteristics to suggest that the Village Creek portion of Jefferson County is composed of other subgroups that clearly fall under the heading

Table 6.1

SOCIODEMOGRAPHIC AND SOCIOECONOMIC CHARACTERISTICS
OF HIGH-POVERTY VILLAGE CREEK NEIGHBORHOODS AS
COMPARED TO JEFFERSON COUNTY, ALABAMA, AND
THE METROPOLITAN UNITED STATES

	Village Creek[a]	Jefferson County[b]	United States[c]
Sociodemographic			
Total Population	13,850	651,525	267,462,000
Percent Black	99%	65%	12.6%
Percent Female-Headed Families With Children under 18	34%	12%	14.3%
Percent 18 Years of Age and Under	28%	20%	21%
Percent 65 Years of Age and Over	18%	14%	11.3%
Socioeconomic			
Percent Persons Living Below Poverty Level	42%	13%	11.8%
Median Household Income	$11,338	$31,105	$17,869
Median Home Value	$30,467	$58,500	$52,100
Percent Vacant Housing Units	18%	8%	6.4%

[a] Data obtained from 1990 Census of Population and Housing (Tracts #7, 8, 33), Birmingham MSA.

[b] Data obtained from 1990 Census of Population and Housing (Jefferson County), Birmingham MSA.

[c] Data obtained from 1996 State and Metropolitan Area Data Book (Metropolitan United States).

of "at risk." For example, the median home value for Jefferson County is $58,500. In comparison, the median home value for the Village Creek census tracts is $30,467. As mentioned earlier, 42 percent of families in these three tracts live below the poverty line. This compares to 13 percent of families living below the poverty line in Jefferson County overall.

Jefferson County is socioeconomically diverse. It contains one of the richest suburbs in the country (Mountain Brook) and some of the poorest neighborhoods in the central city of Birmingham and the state of Alabama. Other poverty indicators (median household income, percent vacant housing units, percent female-headed families with children under the age of 18, and percent of the total population under the age of 18) show the disparity between the larger county and the portion of the Village Creek area identified as underclass.

VILLAGE CREEK HEALTH PROFILE. Perhaps the more important part of the Village Creek story, however, is the health risks associated with residence there. Table 6.2 presents several indicators that help to characterize health risks in Village Creek, Jefferson County, and the United States. Several risks in particular emphasize the unhealthy nature of Village Creek. For example, the percent of infants born to adolescent mothers (ages 10–19) represented 16 percent of all live births in Jefferson County. For the Village Creek area those births represented 30 percent. Approximately 13 percent of all live births in the United States are born to adolescent mothers.

Other indicators of risk are found in the incidence of low birth weights (less than 2,500 grams), percentage of mothers entering prenatal care in their first trimester of pregnancy, and preterm births (less than 37 gestational weeks). Eleven percent of all births in Jefferson County were infants with low birth weights, compared to 19 percent in the high-poverty neighborhoods of Village Creek. Nationwide, the incidence of low birth weight is less than 10 percent. Likewise, 12 percent of live births in the county were preterm, compared to 18 percent in the high-risk neighborhoods of Village Creek. In both cases, these numbers (low birth weight and preterm delivery) were highest among nonwhite residents of Village Creek (Jefferson County Department of Health 1999). Nationally, the percentage of preterm births in 1996 was approximately 11 percent. Finally, the percent of women entering prenatal care in their first trimester of pregnancy in the Village Creek communities was 75 percent. By contrast, in Jefferson County and the United States between 80 percent and 84 percent of women entered prenatal care in the first trimester.

The health profile for Village Creek paints a bleak picture. Not unlike hundreds of neighborhoods around the country, Village Creek is beset

Table 6.2

HEALTH RISKS OF HIGH-POVERTY VILLAGE CREEK
NEIGHBORHOODS AS COMPARED TO JEFFERSON COUNTY,
ALABAMA, AND THE UNITED STATES

Health Risks	*Village Creek*[a]	*Jefferson County*[b]	*United States*[c]
Percent of Births to Adolescents	30%	16%	13%
Percent of Women Entering Prenatal Care in 1st Trimester	75%	84%	80%
Percent Preterm Births (<37 weeks)	18%	12%	11%
Percent Low Birth weight Births (<2500 grams)	19%	11%	7%

[a] Data obtained from 1998 Vital Records Annual Report, Jefferson County Dept. of Health (Tracts #7, 8, 33), Birmingham MSA.

[b] Data obtained from 1998 Vital Records Annual Report, Jefferson County Dept. of Health (Jefferson County), Birmingham MSA.

[c] Data obtained from 1998 Vital Records Annual Report, Jefferson County Dept. of Health (United States).

with problems that are a product of a general environment that is often unresponsive to the needs and concerns of at-risk subpopulations. In addition, the ecological circumstances for many places promote disadvantage because they are located far away from transportation services, receive limited institutional support, present tremendous difficulty in gaining access to health care services, and are located on the periphery of formal service delivery networks (cf. Smith 1988).

The remainder of this chapter explores how contextual characteristics impact health in communities like those found in Village Creek. By applying the earlier theories of health, we examine how place is interrelated with health beliefs, lifestyles, and patterns of risk and protection.

The Ghetto Resident's Dilemma

Is it possible for an isolated subculture residing in a high-risk environment to establish and maintain healthy beliefs and lifestyles inconsistent with its surroundings? The thrust of our argument up to this point would likely be a resounding no. Chapter 4's discussion of health theories provided a strong theoretical argument for why healthy attitudes and lifestyles are difficult to develop in the face of challenging ecological circumstances. The ghetto suffers from a lethal combination of ecological factors that often promote unhealthy attitudes, lifestyles, and risks, with little protection to circumvent negative health outcomes.

As suggested in Chapter 4, several ecological factors play a significant role in influencing the health and well-being of residents. These factors often constrain residents' choices, limit their access to health care services, create unnecessary risks, and nurture beliefs and attitudes that exacerbate an already desperate situation. These communities are the most vulnerable to the influence of these factors because of their social ecology. The inner city's weakened institutional structures, high degree of segregation, absence of weak ties, limited social support, and lack of territorial functioning result in concentrated risks and hazards that Andrulis (1997) refers to as the "urban health penalty."

The inner-city communities suffering most from this penalty are those isolated from the mainstream economy and segregated by race, age, and social class. This penalty intensifies as urban hospitals continue to close and as urban minority physicians remain in short supply, and as the delivery of medical services remains unresponsive to the needs of people unable to pay for their health care. Coupled with this growing penalty of residence is mounting evidence that where one lives is inextricably tied to his or her level of poverty, which in turn affects that individual's physical and mental health (Jargowsky 1997).

Again, even after controlling for individual and family differences, *place matters*. Teenagers who live in poverty-stricken neighborhoods have a greater probability of dropping out of high school, getting pregnant, or having an abortion (Crane 1991; Gephart 1997; Mayer 1991). Minority persons living in poverty are at increased risk to be victims or perpetrators of crime and violence (Elliott, Hagan, and McCord 1998; Levine and Rosich 1996; Reiss and Roth 1993). Poor, inner-city neighborhoods are plagued by higher rates of infant mortality, lead poisoning, respiratory illnesses, cancer, and general mortality than any other place in the metropolitan area (Agency for Toxic Substances and Disease